My Life, My Dreams, My Story

VIRGINIE FORTIN

First published by Ultimate World Publishing 2020
Copyright © 2020 Virginie Fortin

ISBN

Paperback: 978-1-922497-56-7
Ebook: 978-1-922497-57-4

Virginie Fortin has asserted her rights under the Copyright, Designs and Patents Act 1988 to be identified as the author of this work. The information in this book is based on the author's experiences and opinions. The publisher specifically disclaims responsibility for any adverse consequences which may result from use of the information contained herein. Permission to use information has been sought by the author. Any breaches will be rectified in further editions of the book.

All rights reserved. No part of this publication may be reproduced, stored in or introduced into a retrieval system, or transmitted in any form, or by any means (electronic, mechanical, photocopying, recording or otherwise) without the prior written permission of the author. Any person who does any unauthorised act in relation to this publication may be liable to criminal prosecution and civil claims for damages. Enquiries should be made through the publisher.

Cover design: Ultimate World Publishing
Layout and typesetting: Ultimate World Publishing
Editor: Martine Julie

The quotation from Chapter 5 *"Failing to plan is planning to fail"* is taken from Alan Lakein.

The quotation from Chapter 7 *"An average human looks without seeing, listens without hearing, touches without feeling, eats without tasting, moves without physical awareness, inhales without awareness of odour or fragrance, and talks without thinking"* is taken from Leonardo da Vinci.

The quotation from Chapter 7 *"I know that I know nothing"* is taken from Jean Gabin.

Ultimate World Publishing
Diamond Creek,
Victoria Australia 3089
www.writeabook.com.au

Dedication

Firstly, I dedicate this book to myself.

To my parents, for their unconditional love and support. There was not a single parenting book in the world that could have prepared you for me and my eccentricity.

To my brothers and my sister, thank you for always being here for me, as crazy as I could be.

To my children, for choosing me as their mother, thank you.

To my beautiful friends, for their unwavering support and for accepting me the way I am.

To the fathers of my children, thank you for the lessons that each and every one of you has taught me.

Dedicated to everyone who wonders if this story is about them; you have all inspired me, one way or the other.

Contents

Dedication	iii
Contents	v
Introduction	1
Chapter 1: Childhood	3
Chapter 2: School Year and Adaptation	21
Chapter 3: Australia and Work Experience	39
Chapter 4: My Lovers	63
Chapter 5: Motherhood	87
Chapter 6: My Cancer	105
Chapter 7: My Journey, My Legacy	129
About the Author	137
References	139
Testimonials	141
Notes	145

Introduction

My dad is the primary reason for writing this book.

He is not a writer. Mum always double-checks his spelling and grammar. What a team! My love and admiration for them know no bounds. They are my models. Dad wrote his first book about The Camino de St Jacques. It is a journal about the 1700 kilometres he has travelled with mum. They left in April 2006, shortly after celebrating my niece Juliette's twentieth birthday. I flew for the weekend with my son, and they left the following Tuesday. Dad was overweight and not very fit before he left. He shaved everything off, including his hair and his moustache. I had never seen him without his moustache before. Their journey had lasted three months, during which they renewed their vows. The feeling that this book brings me is one of closeness; I can feel their presence even if we are 20,000 kilometres apart. After the Camino, my sister passed away and dad decided to write a booklet about her life. He wanted us to remember her and he inserted a message at the end: "quit smoking."

Retired and busy with mum, dad is always on the lookout for the next project. Mum is more the sporty, aqua gym and walking type of person. Dad loves computers and he is constantly amazed by their potential. It is a shame he cannot always maximise its use, but his children and grandkids are here to help him. Please, guys, do not change anything on his desktop; that will only confuse him.

Virginie

His older brother Pierre has a passion for history. He has put together the whole family tree on my dad's side, the Fortin, as well as my mum's family. Dad had married Monique, who was his brother's wife's cousin. Her name is Yolande.

Dad wanted to write his story. He felt the urge to recollect memories from his childhood, his time in the army during the North African fight for independence, his work, his family and his personal struggles. But he had a dilemma. And that dilemma was Me!

How could he possibly tell my story without hurting my feelings? But telling my own story was my responsibility. I needed to own it, I needed to grow up, so at the age 50, I finally grew. I remember reading somewhere, something in the lines of *"life starts at 50. Before that, it's just a warm-up."*

Now, let me tell you about me and my "warm-up." I am a mother of five children, born from four different fathers, and a stepmother of two. I migrated to Australia when I was 20 years old, I dealt with the Hague Convention regarding the abduction of one of my daughters, lost my sister from cancer and have survived breast cancer myself.

Are you over it yet?

I am not ashamed of my life, but I know my parents and my family might be.

I hope you will enjoy reading this book as much as I enjoyed writing it.

Virginie

Chapter 1

Childhood

～

The first part of this chapter is extracted from my dad's book; it will give you an insight into his thoughts about me and the rest of the family.

On the 30th of September 1969, at 1.30 pm, in the town of Châlons sur Marne, was born "The most beautiful little girl in the world, for the entire year of 1969."
The end of September represents, for the Fortin family and for many others, a meeting point for a multitude of babies. Why? In many cases, it is about starting the year with a new beginning, following the Christmas and New Year holidays. We had several reasons not to deviate from this tradition, and on September 30, 1969, Virginie made her appearance into the world. Upon meeting my aunt Suzanne Fortin, and letting her know the child's future name (Virginie if it's a girl and Alexandre for a boy), she exclaimed: "Well! If it's a girl, good luck. I anticipate she will cause a lot of trouble." She was completely wrong; our daughter

Virginie

was such a joy to live with. By reading the following lines, you will see for yourself.

The existing siblings lived in anticipation of this happy event; everyone was delighted to welcome her. During her early childhood, Virginie posed no difficulties for us, manipulated her grandfather Roger, and got from him whatever she wanted. Like her siblings, she went at the age of 5 to the "La Toussuire" summer camp.

During our stay at Bar sur Aube, she helped us run the bar; she served the customers on roller skates, while holding a tray. I think everyone in the room was waiting for a fall that never came. She was efficient and did not mind hard work. In the middle of this bouquet of praise, we have to find an imperfection, and my biggest disappointment was her decision, after her third year in Business School in Paris and her internship in Australia, to terminate her studies in France, without finishing her fourth year. For me, it has always been a source of shame. It was her decision, and she was of legal age, but in my own personal opinion, I consider a child to be of legal age when he or she can provide for themselves, and that was not the case. But she did not give in.
Like her brothers and sister, she obtained a driving licence and could drive any vehicle. In the dead of winter, she left Bar sur Aube for Dijon without being properly acquainted with her car, a Renault Estafette. In her career as a driver, she has only broken one car door, but was present in the vehicle with Emmanuel during his famous barrel roll on Catherine's wedding day.

I do not wish to approach the period of her love affairs. It is up to her to continue her story; I hope she will find the courage to do it. In the event of a deliberate bankruptcy of her memory, she will always be able to count on mine, so long as I am still a part of the world of the living…
…What does she still have in store for us? I hope she finds the time to write about her life. I encourage her to do it. It will help her heal.

Childhood

In Virginie's veins, flow the genes of generosity, (acquired from her grandmother, France), the qualities of her mother's heart, Monique, and an entrepreneurial spirit and a strong work ethic inherited from her beloved dad. My aunt Suzanne was very wrong; we did not see, but we lived it .

Now, this is an account of myself, from my own personal perspective. I am the daughter of Claude and Monique Fortin. I have an older brother Eric, born in 1962. My two other siblings are the twins Catherine and Emmanuel, born in 1966. The story of my conception is quite funny; on the 31st of December 1968, mum and dad were holidaying in "Les Estables" in the Haute Loire region. Dad was playing cards with some of the noble of the villages. By noble, I mean the mayor and the baker; you get the idea! It was a small town and they were celebrating New Year's Eve. Mum was in bed alone, waiting for her husband to finish his glass of red wine and finally come to bed. He was having too much fun; he had lost track of time. He finally decided to go to bed and dot, dot, dot…..… Mum already had three kids after difficult pregnancies. She had been sick, had needed blood transfusions and had lost her eyesight for a few months. And guess what? To add to her already-existing challenges, here I was, nine months later, born on the 30th of September.

I was born at 1.50 pm in a small town in the Champagne area. I was remarkably close to my grandfather, Roger, who was mum's dad. I could do whatever I wanted; all I had to do was to give him my biggest smile and I just got whatever I asked for. My school years were quite comfortable until I turned 12 years old. I will talk about the later years in the next chapter, but to give you an idea, I attended eight different schools in six different towns over a period of eight years. My older brother Eric used to teach me rock n roll, also known as jive. I was his doll and he made me twist and turn; I have always loved dancing. Whatever he asked me to do, I would just obey. I would even clean his Harley and polish all its wheels. I did so much and yet I felt that he did not even notice me. He used to make me believe silly facts, too. For example, he would tell me that pasta grows on trees and I believed it for so long. No wonder I felt mocked and traumatised. When I was a child, I also had issues pronouncing the word "moufle" which means mitten in French. For some reason, he wanted me to say "moulfe." I did and it always made everyone laugh. I was happy to be the centre of attention.

He is seven years older than me. He also told me that Santa was not real; he showed me where mum and dad were hiding the presents, in the front entrance. I was so disappointed. I suppose I was just an annoying baby sister to him.

While he was a teenager and still at school, it was my duty, every Saturday morning, upon coming back from school myself, to wake him up at 11.30 am for lunchtime. He used to yell and throw pillows at me. This brought up memories of me asking my own kids to wake up their siblings. With Eric, I had to go back upstairs. Every time he did not get up, I felt as if I had failed an important mission. I still remember my parents always on his back, telling him to get up for school; he was waking up at 7.45 am for an 8 am start. He usually had a quick shower and took his motorbike to school. He was so cool. He went to do his compulsory army training for twelve months. He was required to shave his hair. I was shocked when I saw him.

Once when I was at Nancy, he forgot to pick me up from camp. I had just returned from a ski trip to Italy. Back then, I had no mobile phone and no money. My instructor dropped me at his place; nobody was there. No Eric. I could not call my parents as they were 300 kilometres away and Saturday was always a busy day for them. I was carrying my backpack and my ski boots. Everything was heavy. After six hours, I left my bag at my brother's neighbour's apartment and finally decided to call my parents. They announced that I had just become an aunty; Eric was at the hospital for the birth of his daughter Juliette. I walked to one of Eric's friends' house and waited for him there; he finally arrived at 10.30 pm. He was only ten hours late. At least for once in his life, he had a good excuse. Another memory that is still vivid is when I used his phone for hours at a time, to call my boyfriend. I left my brother a nice, big phone bill.

During my school years, my English was not very good and his wife was always very patient with me.

Later in life, when I needed money while I was in Australia, he willingly helped me. He was always here. Not long ago, we had a conversation during which he admitted to not having been "present enough as a brother." The funny side of the story is that we always argue. He has a very sarcastic sense of humour and I have to admit that I am not used to it anymore. It seemed not so long ago that my mum had smacked him because he had made me cry. French people share a unique relationship; we are passionate when we speak. From the outside, it looks as if we are arguing, but in reality, we are not. I love my family dearly.

Now that I am 50, I can say that we have a better relationship after losing our sister to cancer. Eric is now more careful and much more sensitive about my feelings. Back when we were younger, he knew exactly how to push my buttons. But now, I am more assertive and able to tell him whenever I feel hurt. I am sure we all have an Eric in our family. Both Eric and Christine are very present in my life. He is very straightforward. He tells the truth, no matter what and he does not sugar coat anything as your parents normally would. I realised recently that I needed someone like this in my life. Sometimes, he does push it a bit too far and this would often lead him to get into trouble with mum. I think he makes a beautiful grandpa. I purposely wrote the word grandpa here to annoy him, as he wants to be called "boss" by his grandson.

Emmanuel and I are very close. As kids, we were remarkably similar. I just wanted to copy everything he did. He is a beautiful, kind, caring and protective brother and I am his baby sister. I have always loved him very much. He is very different compared to Eric, but still here for me, to this day. He is not much of a talker, but has the biggest heart ever. One day, during our childhood, Emmanuel and I went biking. We were supposed to stay at home and only ride around the house. But of course, we disobeyed and ventured into the street. I fell and scratched my face, my elbows and my knees. Emmanuel had to carry me back to the house, hide me in the kitchen until he could go back and pick up the bikes and everything else we had left behind. He tried to fix me but he could not. We had to lie and told my parents we had been playing in the yard. I used to do a lot of fencing, mainly because my brother was doing it and I just wanted to copy him. I guess I was just, again, being the annoying little sister who just liked to imitate everything her older siblings were doing. When I was twelve years old, Emmanuel left home to pursue his dream. He eventually became the European Champion.

We are so proud of him. His door is always open; his wife Katia always makes me feel welcome. I always feel very happy every time I spend time with them; they are so welcoming. I told all my friends they were always welcome there. I must apologise though; it was very inconsiderate on my behalf, for it wasn't my house. Emmanuel used to pick me up from the airport and drive me back when it was time for me to leave. Their house was a welcoming haven. They always treated us like royalty. I did not realise that he had a life of his own; he never said no. To you Emmanuel: Thank you again for all those return trips to the airport, to the train station, for picking me up to surprise the parents at the farm and for always having your house wide open for me and my acquaintances. My last memory with my brother was in June 2018; I could not decide what to get him for his birthday. I asked him to take the day off for us to spend together, and we went to a spa. I booked massage sessions for us but I did not read the fine print. Not much of a problem, until we were asked to undress for the spa, sauna and the hammam. The personnel were also naked. We laughed; we had never been shy, but having had reconstruction surgery with no nipples, I did not feel that courageous. But somehow, having my brother by my side made me brave and stronger than ever.

My sister Catherine is the complete opposite of me. She is quiet, reserved, does classical dancing, loves reading and is very secretive. She is so beautiful and mystique. She is graceful; even more so during her ballet classes, at which she excelled. Of course, I wanted to try ballet classes too. I only did it for one year. During the end of year show, I was dancing with my classmate; I had two ponytails on each side of my face. During the performance, a lock of hair fell on my face. My arms were up in the air and I could not put my hair back behind my ear. I was blowing it like Popeye, desperately trying to free my face. Despite the music playing, I still heard my parents and grandparents laughing. What an ungracious sight it must have been. After this episode, I refused to go on a stage. I had developed stage fright and I was terrified. In 2013, when my parents came to visit me in Australia, my daughter Mia was also doing ballet. They once went to watch her dance performance and found that she was not interested at all. Mum and dad looked at me and they instantly recognised my skills. Mia and I shared the same genes. She was not destined to be a classical dancer. I remember how Catherine used to pay me to colour her geography map for her homework, to clean her room and make her bed. She was not interested in house chores and hated cleaning or cooking; the exact opposite of me. I really enjoyed ironing, cooking, helping mum or grandpa. I did not like to be on my own, while she could enjoy the company of her own self for hours. She never wanted to play with me. I used to go play with Emmanuel, building train tracks, playing with soldiers and Indian figurines. Catherine was in her own world; I felt I was not a part of it. We always had this competition between us; she liked who I was and I was jealous of how clever and independent she was. Despite being curious about everything, I always needed to be surrounded by people or animals.

I started school at the age of three years old with my best friend Laure, and at the age of 50, I can affirm that our friendship is still strong and growing. She is always here for me, and I hope I am still here for her. Through primary school, our life was simple and very similar. She left for twelve months to go to the United States; she did not have as many husbands or kids as I did or have. She was a better girl than I was. We used to go horse riding together; she was more skilled than me. I also practised fencing. My imagination was fertile. I just wanted to be Zorro; to rebel, fight for justice and do the right thing. Isn't that a characteristic of a Libra? Laure and I were inseparable right until we were ten years old. Her parents were farmers. They also grew asparagus; the big, fat, white ones. I love them so much. We used to play on their property; at the end of it, there was a small river, and we loved playing with tadpoles. We would go back home covered with mud from head to toe; we loved it. Laure and I had a lot of fun together.

One of our dreams was to live in a ranch with horses; this dream has now faded away! We used to have sleepovers at each other's house all the time. One day, she came over to my place and we were full of energy, as usual. I used to own Guinea pigs and we also had a giant slide. We decided to play with them. We took them out of their cage and let them slide; they died of a heart attack! We put them back in their cage, thinking they were tired. My intention was good, don't get me wrong. I just wanted them to have as much fun as we did on the slide. But it did not work out very well.

Laure and I catch up as much as possible; we drive 500 kilometres for coffee or if one of us needs the other. She came to visit me in Australia when I was pregnant with my first child, and we went to Fraser Island with Cyndi. It was so much fun! Laure now has a chalet near Chamonix and we are still catching up to this day. Thirty years later, I took the kids skiing after the painful loss of my sister and my own battle with cancer. I stayed ten days with Laure and the kids; to this day, it is still one of our favourite lifetime memories, both for my kids and family.

The nature of dad's work was such that they needed to entertain their clients; they used to go hunting, catching birds such as pheasants and quails. One day, one of the hunters injured a quail's wings. Usually, hunters break the bird's neck, but this time was different. I pleaded for them to keep her. Turns out they had a lucky day and the truck was full. I held her in my hands, fixed her, and since then, she lives in my grandpa's aviary with the pigeons. We used to have chickens and we also had rabbits because, yes, we ate rabbits too. We raised them for consumption. Maybe it's time to become a vegetarian? The funny thing is, as soon as we gave them a name, we could not get ourselves to eat them anymore. I have always loved animals; I thoroughly enjoy their company. Maybe I should live on a farm.

Mum and dad's neighbour had seven children. He was a surgeon; one of them had goats and all sort of different animals, right in the middle of France. He used to bring all these animals to his father in the garden. I was so excited! His father was not very impressed, as they were destroying his veggie patch. One of them was a donkey. I was five years old at the time; we had a gate between the yard and their house. The donkey was too fast. One day, I decided to pull his tail and he got upset. His hoof landed on my eyebrow, the consequence of which were seven stitches and a lot of headaches.

I was fortunate that the injury was not more serious; maybe this is one of the reasons I am a bit crazy. But yeah, this is me. My parents used to find me regularly outside, sleeping with my dog, a Great Dane. After the downfall of my relationships, maybe I should stick to the company of animals.

My grandparents lived on the same property. They had a small house in front of our home. On our way back from school, we would ring the bell and inquire: "What's for lunch? What's mum cooking?" And if we happened to not like what mum was cooking, we would go straight to my grandma's house. Tuesday night was sleepover night at her's. Such incredible memories with the best grandparents ever!

Virginie

I have very fond memories of Wednesdays, when we had a day off school, going to my grandpa's house to do gardening. When I was six years old, I was gifted the first muguet flower (Lily of the valley - Traditionally in Europe, the muguet is a flower gifted on the 1st of May, for good luck). I had a lot of good fortune throughout my life.

Try to picture me: a tomboy who loved fencing, horse riding and running around in the open. You name it, I did it. I was full of energy. For our holidays, we went to camp for a month. In France, we are not required to wear a uniform at school, but for summer camp, we had to wear dark blue shorts, a yellow t-shirt and a beret with a different coloured inside lining.

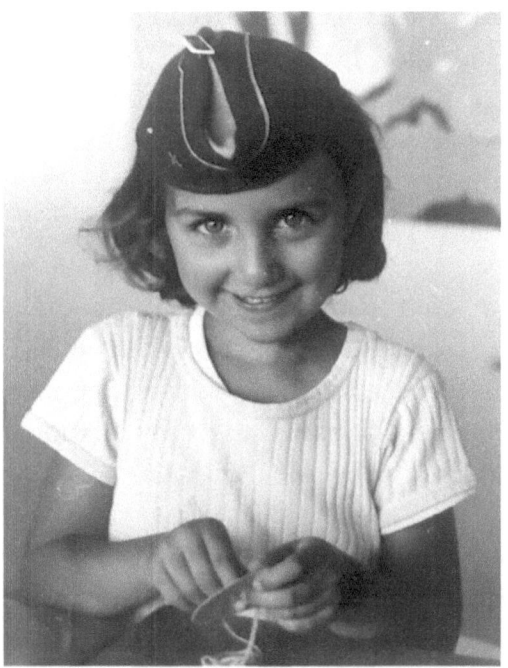

We spent the whole month away from mum and dad, at only five years old. If we had packed some lollies, we had to share it with everyone else. That was the rule. Every night for dinner, we had to finish whatever had been served on our plates. We had to attend church every Sunday, and eat half a grapefruit before lunch. Until this day, I still dislike grapefruits. We went for walks and our afternoon tea was a French baguette with apple purée spread on it. And I remember my brother Eric's joke: "Smell the mashed apples. They smell. Off." They said: "You smell it." And they then smudged the whole French baguette into our face. Nowadays, this is called bullying. I must stress that my two brothers were very protective of their little sister, especially during the "colo," our camp holidays away from home.

Growing up, going to school was a constant. Good old routine. Mum was a housewife. Dad was working in the wallpaper industry. Pretty easy life. One of the things I did not like with the French education system was that you had to do paperwork on the first day of school. You must state your parents' occupation and I now realise how judgemental this whole process was. Whenever I would ask my kids about their friends' parents' job, they would tell me to mind my own business. But what they don't know is that this is what I have been conditioned to think is the norm while growing up: judge the book by its cover. How ironic now, with what is being revealed in this book?

Virginie

We all went to a private school. In France, the title private school differs from the meaning it has in Australia or England. It was more a Catholic school. We did a lot of sports: basketball, fencing, horse riding, diving, swimming and even dancing. For a very long time, I had not realised how lucky we were, how privileged. Fencing and horse riding were expensive hobbies. I did not really understand the value of money. For a very long time, my parents would tell me "You don't have a clue." But I have always believed that if you have the willingness to do something, you can achieve anything. I still have that determination in me. You just have to throw your whole body and soul into it.

Fencing allowed me to travel a lot around France.

Another great memory was going to the movies with my father. We watched three films, and the first one was called "2001 Space Odyssey." Back then, I did not really understand the plot and I still don't. I was six years old when we watched "Jaws" and fifteen when we went to watch Star 80. How funny it is that you remember some films more than others. Of course, I went with mum to see most of Walt Disney's movies! The summer following our trip to the movies to watch "Jaws," we went to Corsica with dad's friends Maurice and Dada. We took the boat out for a swim, and while we were enjoying the water, dad jokingly screamed: "Watch out! A shark!" I knew that we were swimming in the Mediterranean and the probability of coming across a great white shark was impossible, but I froze nonetheless. For an exceptionally long time after this episode, I only swam around the pool. I was unable to go beyond that point, and to this day, I still have a phobia of water. How amazing that such a small event can affect us for the rest of our lives. I can go bungee jumping and even water rafting with ease, but when I went diving on the Great Barrier Reef, I ended up emptying my oxygen tank in a record time.

One of my uncles was separated from his wife, and on Wednesday afternoons, we were assigned to look after my cousins Caroline and Isabelle. I could not go horse riding anymore as I had to entertain them. I was so upset about it. My mum told me I was selfish and she was probably right, but I still think it was unfair for me to have to sacrifice my sport to look after someone else's children. It was not for too long, but to me, it felt like it was forever.

Between school, birthday celebrations, weekend sport, basketball, fencing and swimming, our life was busy. Having pizza on Friday nights, after fencing, had almost become a tradition. Sometimes on the weekend, we would go to a nice restaurant. I did not realise at the time that going to beautiful restaurants was a privilege. We had to behave ourselves and sit properly and straight, no elbows on the table, mouths closed and no eating with our fingers. My parents even taught us how to peel prawns with a knife and fork, and how to eat snails with the proper cutlery. We took the instructions with enthusiasm, as usual. I thought everybody was doing it. Mum and dad always made it a point to teach us good manners; for them, it was a vital tool for succeeding in life. I remember a couple of comments during our trips to the restaurant where I probably embarrassed my parents. One of our special Christmas dishes is the "foie-gras," and no, it is not JUST a pâté! You may think it is animal cruelty, whether it be the farmed force-fed duck or the goose which had its whole liver removed. That explains its name, literally translated as "fat-liver." It is a delicacy. It is expensive.

So here we were, at this nice restaurant and I decided to order "foie-gras." Mind you, it was summertime, not Christmas, and I was six years old. My father discreetly told the waiter to give me a "pâté de grives," literally translated as "thrush pâté." During lunch, they asked me how was my "foie gras," and I told them it was the best "foie gras" I had ever eaten. Another funny episode happened when we ordered some "flageolets." The nickname for this bean is "pêteux," which means "make a fart." Now try to imagine a Michelin Star restaurant; quiet, hardly any noise. You were not supposed to raise your voice there. As soon as I saw them served on the table, I said, at the top of my lungs: "look at the farting beans." It was an embarrassing moment for my parents, but they smiled and patiently explained that it was an inappropriate thing to say, especially in public.

Upon moving out of the family house, my world fell apart. Dad was made redundant from his job. After the war, there had been a significant expansion in the reconstruction industry, but the demand was getting scarcer and scarcer. Dad has done a wonderful job of explaining this period of hardship in his book, in his own words. It is his story, after all. Thank you, dad, for having shared it with us.

I was young when it happened. From my innocent perspective, dad had just stopped working, and we had to move from the house where I was born. I was genuinely fortunate; I have such vivid and precious memories. I loved our old house; the furniture was Louis 16, there were matching wallpaper and marble side tables and leather desks. The following years were a time of adaptation. Before dad lost his job, we used to go to Corsica every summer for four weeks, and we also went skiing in winter. I felt blessed and fortunate to have been on those holidays. My older brother, Eric, was a regular at the summer camp called "La Toussuire." He went from the age of five and probably until he turned fifteen. I only went there for a couple of years. After that, the whole family went to Corsica with our family friends Maurice and Marie-Claude.

Childhood

In 2018, I went back to Corsica, after 30 years. The place had hardly changed, and I met with friends who were only 12 when I left. We were now over 50, and were still able to recognise each other. How amazing! It was surreal. That was all thanks to my parents and Marie-Claude, who had organised a return down memory lane. I spent four magnificent weeks in the company of mum and dad. Time flies and while there, I came to the realisation that they can leave us at any time. It was the best holidays ever.

Chapter 2

School Year and Adaptation

I had a privileged childhood, and the beginning of my school life went by without any major issues. Then, dad was made redundant and changes upon changes started to happen, one after the other. I love to refer to movies, and this one was called "Inside Out."

There are quite a few differences between the school system in France and the one in Australia. In France, a child goes to "maternelle" or kinder from three to five years old, until they are ready to attend primary "school" for grade 1. This is followed by elementary school until grade 5, and "college" from grade 6 to grade 9, after which you can choose different pathways; technical (TAFE) or classical for your Baccalaureate in year 12. From year 10 to 12, it is called "Lycée." You need to take the French Baccalaureate exam in year 11, the marks of which count for the following year. In year 12, you have to sit for a final exam.

In **June 1982**, after grade 9, Emmanuel was allowed to graduate to grade 10 but when my parents mentioned that their son intended to enrol in the "sports-études" (Elite sport and study program), the school had a sudden change of mind. My mum had to appeal to the Education Department, and Emmanuel was finally able to pursue his educational goals. Because of the clashes that happened regarding Emmanuel, my parents decided to choose a different school for me and in **September 1982**, I was enrolled at the College Perrot d'Ablancourt. I was 13 years old, in grade 8. I was an average student overall, but I excelled in Maths and Science, despite having transitioned from a Catholic school to a public one. It was quite a bad decision to be honest; the new school turned out to be a jungle. Some of the students were nearly 16. If you are younger than 16 years old, you cannot be expelled because education as such is compulsory. But throughout the year, six kids were expelled. The whole class was regularly in detention, and the entire class did not have maths classes for a while as our teacher had a mental breakdown. She had lost her father, and some of the students had written on the board if "she had found her dad." They even threw her bag through the window; we were on the 3rd floor! Under these extreme circumstances, our principal had to be present while we had class. I survived without much damage, except losing one year as I had to redo the whole year level.

The only good thing during this time was meeting my friend Françoise; she had six siblings and her mum was from England. When we were thirteen, her mum asked us to address her as "vous." A little bit of a French lesson: in standard contemporary Modern English, **"you"** stands for **both singular and plural**. In French, "tu" stands for singular "you" and "vous" for plural. But "vous" can also be applied in a singular mode to show respect. For example, if you wish to speak to a person older than you, or to your boss, using the "tu," you need to ask them if that's ok first, even if they happen to be 20 years younger than you.

Back in the days, Françoise's parents organised "disco nights," and my older brother Eric was friends with the older siblings of the family. Disco for the little ones (11 to 14 years old) was from 2 pm to 5 pm, for the older kids (15 to 18 years old) from 5 pm to 8 pm, and the adults "partied the whole night." It was such an organisation; always a big table and everybody was welcome. Françoise's mum was the cook, and all the kids had a special job assigned. What a great childhood memory! In 1984, we went on holidays together to the farm, where we collected fresh cow's milk. We would let it set in a big bowl and in the morning, we would scoop the cream that had collected at the top. After their fathers' death, they moved closer to Paris, as Europe became a central meeting place for the siblings. I lost contact with them but maybe one day, we will meet again.

The year 1982 is also memorable because my brother Emmanuel qualified for the European Fencing Championship. He left Corsica to go to Spain while he was only 16. He eventually won and went on to become the European Champion. He left the following year for Henin Beaumont. After that, I did not see much of him anymore.

September 1982.

I had to redo my grade 8. My parents transferred me to an old Catholic Boys school that Eric used to attend. It was the first year the school had become a co-educational one. There

Virginie

were only four girls per class. By that time, I was more used to being around boys as I was a tomboy by nature, and played fencing with them. My first detention was handed by my History teacher. He did not like me as I was related to Eric. On the first day of school, while doing the roll call, he asked me if I was Eric's sister. As soon as I replied in the affirmative, he instantly put me in a mental box labelled "trouble maker." I was in the same class as Laure's cousin, Benoit, and we had so much fun. One day, I laughed so hard that the teacher had to ask me to leave the class. Even then, I still could not hold myself. The following day, we had history class with this same teacher. Benoit was standing in front of me, waiting to enter the classroom, and I decided to trip him. The poor guy was sent to the vice-principal. Meanwhile, the teacher had started doing the roll and he asked me whether I had an excuse for having left the class the day before. I replied: "Of course not! You are the one who sent me out. I did not have any other choice!" I also ended up being sent to the vice principal. Upon reaching his office, I witnessed Benoit trying his best to explain his case, explaining that I had tripped him. It was now my turn to be called by the vice-principal, who was a priest. He asked me the reason for which I was sent to him. After telling my version of the story, I was handed one hour of detention for being sent out of the class the day before, and another hour for tripping my friend. I started getting worried about dad, who was not going to be impressed by my punishment. I could not get away with it. The priest told me that I was an "effrontée," (sassy with 2 SS), and without prior thinking, I told him : "Yes I am, and you spell it with 2 FF!" It used to be a joke in the Fortin's residence. But not at school, where my comment was inappropriate. And zoom! Another hour of detention. Three hours in one go, but it went quite well. I think dad was able to recognise a bit of himself in me; with the inability to hold

School Year and Adaptation

my tongue. During this time, I became friends with Yves, and later on, we would both live in Paris. He was my dance partner. Throughout year 8, my parents encouraged me to try different extracurricular options, such as Latin or learning how to use a typewriter. I did not really enjoy having to do all these extras, but they eventually proved to be very useful later in life.

1983. Dad was made redundant. He was always at home. He was going to change his career, our lives were about to change, from mum being a housewife, us having a privileged life, to no more practicing horse riding, no more fencing, no more Corsica, and no more skiing in winter. The only positive thing I remember from that time was my dog VIP, a mini poodle. He was my confidant.

September 1984.

My parents became business owners, after purchasing a cafe. I suddenly went from a privileged status to one where I was constantly being judged by my teachers. According to their opinion, my parents were under-achievers and had a bad reputation, because they were now operating a business. We moved to Bar sur Aube in September, shortly after Eric's wedding.

My sister and I started school, while staying at a hotel. From our beautiful house, which we took for granted, we were now headed to inhabit an old, cold place, with no fireplace, no beautiful bathroom, and no warmth. The dining room was on the second floor and the kitchen on the bottom floor. Prior to this big change, I was living in a comfortable bubble, shielded from the outside world. I quickly started feeling restricted, unable to thrive in this new life devoid of sports, fencing club and horse riding. While I was thirteen years old, I was diagnosed with depression. To this day, I have a lot of admiration and respect for my parents who never used the word "depressed." Rather, they just told me it was a normal feeling to have, as my world and my body were undergoing tremendous changes.

I think that as kids, Eric and I spent a lot of time in hospital. A quick overview of these unfortunate episodes would be: At 5 years old, splitting my eyebrow as a result of an encounter with a donkey. 8 years old: a cyst behind my knees, requiring sixteen stitches. 12 years old: falling from show jumping and splitting a vertebrae. I needed two years of physio, had to wear braces and afterwards, had issues with my sciatic nerve. After our arrival in Bar sur Aube, I had to take medication for the depression. I felt better after two weeks, and I did not need it anymore. Mum and dad respected my choice, but kept the box of medication handy, just in case.

School was horrible, and I was unhappy. I was learning to be independent. I wanted to achieve so many things: go to boarding school and run away.
I have only two memories from Bar sur Aube. The first one was the weekend of the 29 to 30 September 1984. I was becoming a teenager. I told my parents I was organising a birthday lunch for mum. She was born on the 29th of September and I was born on the 30th; I happened to be her 30th birthday present. I remember the menu very clearly: smoked salmon and toast, green beans and "gratin dauphinois" (potato bake), lamb roast, and a cake I had purchased from the pâtisserie. When it was time to eat, we all sat at the table. The roast and the "gratin" were not cooked; I had tried to program the oven but it was a complete fail. I did

not want to ask for help; I wanted to do it all by myself. I was too proud, too independent, too stubborn.

Usually, for all our birthdays, mum and dad always had grand celebrations. Dad used to send mum red roses according to her age, and he used to buy me a mini Japanese garden. I always felt so lucky as I was the only one to receive a special present from dad. The other kids received the usual gift that mum would get from the family. I think when dad sent roses to mum when she turned 40, she did not have enough vases to put them around the house. On this particular birthday, mum did not have time to buy me a present. Keep in mind that she had four kids, one of whom just got married, one was living in Northern France with his sports academy, and the last two girls were starting a new school. My parents had just started a new business, and still had to financially provide for all of us. On this day, from a Pulco note pad (advertised note pad given by supplier), she wished me a happy birthday and as a present, whatever I wanted. This was the first time I saw my dad crying. We all cried and laughed together; this birthday was unique; it was the beginning of a completely different life.

The second memory I have of that specific time is of how rude I was with my mum, as a result of which dad had to chase me in the staircase; I ended up getting my last smack.

At the café, it was the first time I saw my parents arguing. Women at the bar did flirt openly with dad in front of mum, and I think she was jealous. Men would do the same with mum. Dad did not feel the need to explain anything; to him, it was nonsense, and he did not need to justify himself either. My parents told us that, according to the statistics, couples who own a café have a higher probability of divorce

These clients at Bar sur Aube wanted to impress the world, their talk was immoral and went against all the values that my parents had ever taught me. One day, I felt in a daring mode and told these customers to try to use their brain and think. Dad discreetly tried to discourage me from arguing with them, but I kept talking back. He eventually had to send me to my room, telling me I was rude. I was so upset; he came back to explain that they were the clients, and as such, they are always right. Should we always speak the truth or become businesspeople and pretend that everything is fine? Becoming a teenager was already a tedious process, and I also had to deal with the fact that mum and dad had to compromise on certain things for the sake of their new business. They were trying to find their way, they were completely out of their comfort zone. Eric had just married his wife, and was still a student. Emmanuel was well into his sport and study program, and Catherine was in year 12. She was a beautiful young woman, who was being courted by all the boys from our small town. She was the star of the city, a trophy to be won. Who was going to get her? I was the baby, going through puberty; I did not understand that my parents had so much to deal with. As a mum myself, going through tremendous changes and completely outside of my comfort zone, it is now my duty to remind my kids and myself; you do not know what you do not know, until you have to go through it yourself.

A new and frightening world opens up to us when we learn to lie. "The customer is always right." This sentence played on repeat in my mind. I am baffled. What is going on? What is happening to our lives? How can you keep being true to yourself in a world that encourages you to compromise your values?

School Year and Adaptation

September 1985, Cour Notre Dame.

Mum and dad were always busy. I wanted to move to Nancy to a boarding school. But there were no boarding schools there as such; it was a convent that accommodated young ladies. The students were private ones, as well as other kids who found themselves caught up in the social system. They did not have anywhere else to go. Both parents were either dead or in prison. They were outcasts. One of my roommates never wanted to leave her room. She was severely depressed. No wonder why; one day, she had found her father at home. He had hanged himself. As we became friends, I realised that we were on the same medication. I cried; I did not know I had depression. This disease was still a taboo in France and it was also shameful for my family. One of the girls in the convent told me to toughen up. She helped me put things in perspective; at least I had someone and somewhere to go back to. She had nothing and no-one, she was just stuck there. And here I was, complaining. Once again, my little bubble of comfort was busted. Moving on from there, I attended a private all-girls school. They were so mean, and it was constant bullying. I was constantly told that: "I was stupid, I was nothing." In year 10, I wanted to study Maths and Science, but the school recommended the Technical pathway for me. It consisted of Accounting as a subject. I felt like an idiot and remembered Michel Sardou's song about "Bac G" Baccalauréat Gestion (Accounting); referred to as the cheap education. But I was determined to get to the Science path. I repeated my year 10 and was finally allowed to study the subject of my choice. By that point, I was already two years behind most of the kids in my class. I reminded myself that if I persisted on this track, I would be 25 by the time I finished year 12. I finally decided to pursue the Technical path, "Bac G," the cheap and not so glamorous option.

Virginie

1986 came with a change of school and a change of accommodation. I was living without my parents at Ghislaine's house, next to the train station in Nancy. All my friends were older and already in year 12. I was still completing grade 10, had started fencing again and was training hard. I was determined to find a new purpose. I wanted to be fully in charge of my life. One should not wait for the adventure to happen; we had to work to make it happen.

I was attending St Elisabeth, a private school. On Friday afternoons, we had a Biology class between 4 pm and 5.30 pm. Recess was at 5 pm, and for only five minutes. After a couple of weeks, I decided it was a waste of time; I left the class at 5 pm and by the end of the term, everybody else decided to follow. Of course, the teacher noticed, and gave me my second detention. I deserved it, as it had been three months since I had missed the last thirty minutes of class. I worked and partied hard. I missed my parents. They were always too busy for me. No more holidays to look forward to, as school holidays were the busiest time of the year for their business.

School Year and Adaptation

1987. I decided to go live closer to my parents at St Dizier. I was still practising fencing outside boarding school. The way the system worked was simple: You eat at school, but you reside with a neighbouring family for year 11. In year 12, I had my own apartment. I found my voice, went in detention, missed my bus, hitch hiked my way back home; I was adventurous as ever! I supposed my parents were too busy to notice. I was a bit of a rebel, but a lovely kind of rebel. A new Maître d'Armes in St Dizier used to drive me back to my apartment. I never thought anything of it. I was practising fencing since I was five years old. It was a safe place to be for me. But one night, he conducted himself in an inappropriate way; he was having sinister intentions. I was shocked because he was married. I had always felt secure, and most of my friends were boys. And what a great friendship I shared with Didier, Jean-Baptiste and Vincent. I related the incident to Maître Barsacq. He told me I was not a kid anymore, and that I now have to be aware of the power of flirting. A couple of years later, Philippe Barsacq passed away; he left behind his wife and three beautiful kids.

I was also preparing for the National Championship. Usually, I did not have the drive to win or the killer instinct; I was just happy to be where I was; fit, catching up with my friends, and used to running thirty kilometres a week. During this championship, I was really angry with my Maître d'Armes. I resented him, I was upset that I did not feel safe anymore in the fencing world which had been my safe zone. I was doing well during this competition, my coach was encouraging me, but I did not trust him. The more he encouraged me, the more I disliked him. I became so angry that I ended up injuring myself, breaking a small bone in my heels. This may be the reason I was so successful at this championship; I had the killer instinct then. I always preferred the beauty of fencing than the actual result of the competition; I was so used to winning as a child. For a very long time, I was the only one in my category. I was so young, and I used to compete with people older than myself. I would still win their division plus mine on the same day. On that day, I finished 16th at national level.

1988.

The year of my Baccalaureate. So many different subjects, and the prerequisite to pass was to score 10 out of 20. Your average was determined by each subject having a different coefficient, depending on your study option; Accounting, Maths, Economics, or Literature. In year 11, you study French in depth, the scores of which are added to the Baccalaureate total at the end of year 12. You can be an outstanding student for the whole year and still fail on the exam. I scored 2 out of 20 for the writing component of my French subject; I failed it completely. When I showed my draft to my sister Catherine, she expressed the same fears as me. But somehow, in the oral exam, I managed to get 12 out of 20. I had always been a better speaker; how ironic that I am now writing my own book. It does not feel like writing to me though; I am just externalising my thoughts on paper. Back to the Baccalaureate, I did well in Maths, Accounting, Economics and Sports. English was catastrophic. I must admit that I have a fear of expressing myself in writing. As a family, one of our hobbies was to play "Trivial Pursuit." A well-known fact in my family: Virginie would never get the plastic wedge. She was the clown, the master of the illiterates. I did not enjoy reading; I was very active, always on the move, dancing, partying and planning the next project, the next travel. During year 11 and 12, I had a boyfriend; his name was Nicolas and his nickname was Nounours. He was a beautiful soul, and was about to go to

School Year and Adaptation

England, to Wimbledon, in June. I persuaded my parents that I needed to go too, to improve my English. At that point, I was 14 marks behind and I needed to make up for it in order to pass my Baccalaureate. I booked my ticket before the make-up oral session. My parents were horrified. Maybe they lacked faith in me. What would happen if I did not pass the first round? But I trusted myself somehow and believed in my abilities to succeed. And I was right. I did succeed and was awarded my Baccalaureate. What was next? I was unsure about which study and career path to choose; BTS, IUT, Business School, or University? It was a hard choice. I ended up applying for a course called "Prep HEC," which is a preparation for the entry exam into High Business School. Some of these schools are very prestigious. I would not define myself as an academic per se. I am far from being stupid; I just like to pursue my own interests.

1989.

19 years old and the adventure was just starting. I passed my driving test and got my licence after only two weeks of lessons. I went on my last holidays to Corsica with my parents; I was driving mum's convertible there. She was always very scared, often getting out of the car and walking. She felt safer that way. After the holidays, I was due to start another "Prepa" in Dijon. I had to arrange new accommodation. Mum and dad let me borrow their Renault "Estafette." The two-seater was not as sexy as the convertible, but it had four wheels and a roof, not even a radio or a heater. I left for Dijon. The reason I had a car was because I had to travel 140 kilometres, which would take me eight hours by train and 2 hours by car. As a parent now, I understand the trust they put in me. On my second trip in my new car, I was picking up a friend on the way, and the fuel gauge

never worked. We were 20 kilometres away from Dijon, we had run out of petrol and the car did not lock. We decided that I would stay in the car, while my friend would hitchhike to Dijon, to his grandparents' house and come back with petrol. I was supposed to arrive by 8 pm. I arrived at midnight, tried to find a car park, and got stuck between cars. The police arrived; my bumper bar was locked with another bumper. I was exhausted, my heart racing, very worried. I did not know what to do, and had already given up when the policemen helped me to unstuck my vehicle. I inquired on the process of leaving my details, in case I had damaged someone else's car. They laughed and told me the driver was not supposed to park there and they should be happy to not be getting a fine. I finally called mum and dad to let them know I was safe.

"Prepa" was hard; my scores were well under average. I wouldn't say I enjoyed studying there, although I did meet some terrific people. Unfortunately, I failed to keep in touch because, after four months, I decided to move to Paris. I was running away, once again.

I was still in a relationship with Nicolas. By then, I was renting a small bedroom with a shower, sink, toilet, and a stove in the bathroom. I used to eat at the university's restaurant. We used the Renault Estafette for a couple of ice-skating trips. We had two people at the front and another ten at the back. Highly illegal stuff.

Another scary adventure happened one Sunday night. Upon coming out of the shower, someone knocked on my door. I thought it was one of my neighbours, as you needed a code to enter the building. It happened to be a stranger. He ended up knowing everything about me: my timetable, where my friend

School Year and Adaptation

lived, my boyfriend's name, the school I was attending. He had forced his way into my apartment while I was in a bathrobe. He sat down. He talked and I listened. I was compassionate, and when he had finished talking, he left. It was scary, but I managed to stay calm and serene. I felt protected.

While at Dijon, some business schools were promoting themselves. If you happened to miss your orientation, you could start the year in February, with six weeks of intense class with only 15 students, while catching up with your current year. The student who begins in September has 6 weeks of business placement. We were expected to do practical work during our summer holidays. It sounded very tempting. One of the schools to offer this program was the ESIAE, Ecole Supérieure Internationale Administration des Entreprises. I wanted to try a couple of schools and each time you sat for an exam, you had to pay a significant fee. Mum and dad were advising me to try one of them and see if I was comfortable. For this first exam, I went to Paris to my brother Emmanuel and his wife Katia's house. I did succeed and here I was, moving to Paris. My Auntie Suzanne, the one who featured in my name-choosing episode, found a lady who lived in Boulogne Billancourt who was renting a room. She was referred to as a "bourgeoise," a lady. Mum and dad upgraded my car from an Estafette to an Austin Metro. Bigger size than a Mini. At 50 years, one of my dreams is still to own a Mini Cooper. But is it really a necessity?

I loved the new school and the teachers. My English teacher believed in me. Nicolas was on his way to Paris; he had rented a studio at Issy Les Moulineaux, and we eventually moved in together. I left the lady's house at Boulogne Billancourt, and hid it from my parents. I was thoroughly enjoying my studies and my love life was excellent. I was both working and studying hard. I went to a camp with ESIAE to complete a leadership course. While I was there, my great uncle Gabriel passed away. For the first time since I had moved to Paris, my parents called the lady in Boulogne. She told them how I had left her house six months ago. We did not have a mobile phone at the time; the only contact number my parents had was my work one. They called and left a message.

Back home, I was in big trouble. I had to leave immediately for Epernay and explain myself. Deception and lies. What were my intentions? Marrying Nicolas? I felt a bit pressured, to be honest. My grandma was very supportive. Mum and dad listened to the million reasons I had for living with Nicolas. If we argued, it would be harder to get through it because we would be sharing the same space. It is so easy to slam the door and go back to your apartment when you have your own place to live. My parents insisted that I move out. I semi agreed, but this partial agreement involved a lot of couch surfing, mainly at Nicolas's. I will talk about my lovers in another chapter.

During my second year in Paris, I had to go overseas for training. My two choices were South Africa and Australia. Dad did not allow me to go to South Africa because of the raging Apartheid. I went to the Australian Embassy; they were holding a competition and the winner would receive a return ticket from Paris to Sydney. I won the second prize, 1000 French Francs, which at the time was the equivalent of $250. The airfare was $2500. I was so excited. The only issue I faced was that I was required to have a signed contract with an Australian-based company in Australia in order for them to issue a traineeship visa. Without the agreement, there would be no visa. The lady who owned the agency that helped students go study in Australia told me she could try to get me a working holiday visa, usually reserved

School Year and Adaptation

for members of the Commonwealth. She was also enrolling me for some courses at UTS (the University of Technology, in Sydney). All I would need to do was to find a traineeship in a business when I arrived. The school allowed me to go as I had a working holiday visa; I was the first person to go to Australia without a job already secured. I was 20; and could only speak extraordinarily little English. I arrived in Sydney. I had my visa, my accommodation for six weeks and 1000 French Francs per month. I was now on my own. Australia, here I come.

Chapter 3

Australia and Work Experience

Australia, here I am.

First Trip: May 1991 to February 1992.

I arrived in Pagewood, NSW at the end of May. I was staying with a host family with four other students. I was from Paris and arrived in Sydney in 1989. It was so quiet compared to Paris. You could take a ferry anytime; it felt like a holiday. The weather was so beautiful. I spent much of my time exploring, appreciating the beauty of every new thing. I love Sydney; it is a lovely city. It is clean, smells beautiful and is full of wonderful places such as the Botanical Garden, the Rocks, and the Sydney Harbour bridge. What a magical place! The days were great, but

Virginie

I quickly started feeling cold. I had only packed summer clothes. I was amazed by everything; it was so different from Europe, where I had travelled; I went to Spain, Italy, England, Scotland, Germany, Belgium, Hungary and Switzerland. I feel lucky to have witnessed the beauty of these countries too. I am a half-full cup type of girl. As per my mother's saying, I see the good in everything. One thing that surprised me was the number of different churches; Anglican, Baptist, Unity, Christian, and many more. I was bewildered. As far as I am concerned, based on the values that I was raised with, the house of God can be a temple or a mosque. I go there to pay my respect, to talk to Him or to immerse myself in the stillness and the serenity of His presence.

I lost my three grandparents within a year, and the hardest loss of all was my Papi, mum's dad. They lived next to us, at Avenue de Metz. He was my guardian angel, he always had my back. I was always the one to receive his first "Brin de Muguet" (Lily of the valley) on the 1st of May. We believe it brings luck. I also always got the first strawberry he picked; the only fruit I loved eating. During his funeral, I had a nervous laugh, a giggle. Please do not judge me, but I actually saw him behind his coffin; he was also laughing and telling me he was ok. When I went to this church in Pagewood in Sydney, I saw him again. He reiterated that he was ok, and that everything was going to be ok for me. I believed him. Life so far had been a roller coaster, but I still wanted to hold on to the idea that it was going to be ok.

At the University of Technology in Sydney (UTS), I met Xavier and Karen who were from New Caledonia. We became buddies, and 30 years later, we are still friends. We don't see each other as much as we would like to, but they are always there for me.

Australia and Work Experience

I moved to Leichhardt, and found a job in Camperdown at S&G Advertising, a Direct Marketing company. The pay was commission-based, and my parents thought I had joined a cult. They urged me to find a real job, but all the French companies I applied at were not willing to pay; they expected me to gain experience prior. I needed to find money; I could not just be a waitress forever. Ideally, my job would have to be relevant to my training. I regularly checked the newspaper for job advertisements. I did not speak English fluently, but when I saw this job at S&G Advertising, it sounded right to me. I did ask them probably ten times to spell the address of the street. At the time, I was mixing the letters "e" and "i," and "j" and "g." The English alphabet was so confusing, and for them to constantly have to spell "A for Alpha and P for Peter" was just a living nightmare. I was resourceful though and very proactive; I borrowed a street map to find my way around. I will deliberately omit how confused I was between the number "eighty" and "eighteen." It was quite an interesting episode; I went in for the interview, and I got the job. They must have been in desperate need of staff!

Virginie

At work, everybody was called by their first name. It was a significant change for me. Work setting in France is very formal. But in Sydney, I found the system to be very American-styled; there was a lot of singing, screaming and jumping. I still remember their motto: "Juice, Attitude and Motivation." If my children ever asked me how to navigate our way to go somewhere, I used to tell them: "Juice, Attitude and Motivation." They probably thought I was crazy, or maybe just French.

Our feelings were taken into consideration; we were exposed to a lot of inspirational speakers and personal development workshops, but I did not really understand anything of it at the time. We were encouraged to oversee our destiny and set our own goals. I loved it. It was hard work, but they taught me how to be in control of my life. The team was excellent; the multicultural people I met were fantastic.

But oh, my God! At times, I did wonder how I was going to sell those cards. I learnt by heart what I was supposed to say. I spent the first couple of days with someone who was training me. I was selling an advertising card for $20, promoting a restaurant. Every time I would sell one, I would earn $5. The first week, I sold one or two a day. I was making $10 per day, spending them in food and public transport. It was a nightmare. I think most people were buying it because they felt sorry for me. Often, I asked them to write down their question. I also had a dictionary to help me check the words I did not understand. I remember saying to them: "You just need to read it; it's a good deal!"

I needed to speed up my game. I worked every night looking for new words in the newspaper to build my vocabulary. The company was supportive. They were helping me. There were a lot of young people; very enthusiastic, optimistic, with a great attitude. We were encouraged to believe in our dreams. This was entirely new for me; my parents thought I was in a sect; they were concerned because I seemed so excited. It was an exceedingly tricky beginning; but by the end, my charming personality and my French accent became a weapon.

I remember this promotion. It was a beautiful restaurant in Auburn, NSW. The decor was welcoming, there was a white tablecloth and a fireplace. It was at the back of a famous pub. What I did not know was that the pub had a bad reputation. The waitresses were serving topless. Nobody else liked the promotion but I loved it, as I did not fully understand all the negative aspects of it, or the slamming of doors. I was smiling; it was a number game. I became a good salesperson.

On another occasion, I did well in sales, and I had to talk in front of the group. I was shy and I just said: "I had a lot of fun with Willy." Of course, everybody started to laugh. I did not get it at the time. I was genuinely talking about Willy, who was a colleague of mine. Let's not mention all the funny expressions or the sounds that ever came out of my mouth; this could be the focus of another book.

S&G was expanding, and because of it, I did a lot of interstate travel. We went to Melbourne for a rally with the group. Shane was the Managing Director of S&G. He was opening an office in Adelaide. He suggested I should go with the team. It was convenient, as I was planning to travel with Karen and Xavier. They were going to see the Grand Prix, and Adelaide was our meeting point. We drove from Melbourne to Adelaide. I worked and visited Adelaide for a month; it was beautiful. Shane lent me his car to go to the beach; I parked at the wrong place and had three fines totalling $370. I was devastated and ashamed. I told Shane about it, and went to the Department of Transport where they waived two of the fines. I still had to pay $90. I appreciated their kindness.

I did have to send a monthly report to my school back in France. The office did not have a fax or email. Shane drove me to a hotel to send my fax. At the reception, they asked me if I was French, as the Ligier Car Racing Team was staying there. They requested my phone number. Philippe Streiff, part of the Ligier team, called the office and we went out for dinner. I was not personally interested by the Grand Prix, but Karen and Xavier had a three-day full-day pass. So Philippe gave us 3 VIP passes for the race, and we went to the MacLaren and Williams parties. It was a memorable experience. I was extremely fortunate.

Shane was meeting up with his school friends, the Black Magnets, to go to the Grand Prix. It was a yearly trip. I was staying with Shane and the team from the office. During this trip, I kissed Shane. I did not want to think about it, as I was still with my boyfriend Nicolas at the time.

I left Adelaide and flew to Alice Springs with Karen and Xavier. When we arrived, we hired a car. Catastrophe! My budget did not take into consideration the price of petrol in the Northern Territory. It was so expensive! Back in Sydney, the price was $0.25 and over there, they charged over $1 in the town centre. We spent two days in Alice Springs, and then drove towards Uluru/Ayers Rock. We did what many tourists did; we stopped to take several photos of Mount Conner, thinking it was Uluru. The local called it "Fool-Uru." We went to Kata Tjuta/The Olgas; we were chased by emus, we went to Kings Canyon, we slept in the car, and we scared ourselves. It was the trip of a lifetime.

Australia and Work Experience

We were driving a four-wheel drive, and it was a new model but 30 years ago, we had to swap the fuel tank manually. Let us say it took us sometime to figure out how to do it, studying the user manual in English. Our English was bad, and we were glad they had pictures, but what mattered was that we brought back some fantastic memories.

After our beautiful experience, it was time for me to fly to Darwin. The departure time was changed and I missed my flight. They could not contact me on time, as I did not have a mobile phone, or an email; they were not as common back in the days. We were using public phones, telegrams and letters.

Whenever I travelled around Australia, I tried to book flights in order to arrive around early afternoon, to give me time to find a backpackers' hostel to stay. Unfortunately, on this occasion, I arrived in Darwin late in the evening. Most of the backpackers' accommodations were full. When I eventually found one, I was given a room of 10, with nine guys. I was a bit apprehensive, but they were friendly. The experience of backpacking was great, except that I had my jean stolen from the clothesline. I went on a beautiful trip for three days in Kakadu National Park. I went horse riding, galloping with kangaroos, and I slept underneath the stars in the bush. It was magical; it was my dream coming true. It was beautiful; I went to see the crocodiles, ate some buffalo burger, tasted crocodile and emu. I met some possums at the backpackers', and I drank a lot of beer. We played volleyball on the beach, and I got sunburnt, and then I flew back to Cairns. I had very little money left. Between buying petrol in the Northern Territory and my trip to Kakadu, I was broke. All my flights were already paid: Adelaide - Alice Springs – Darwin - Cairns - Brisbane, and back to Sydney.

Virginie

When I arrived in Cairns, I was on a budget. I went to a backpackers' accommodation, and we found a pub where we could eat a slice of pizza for $1. While I was there, the pub was holding a horizontal bungee competition. They attached two people with an elastic to their waists, and you had to be the first one to reach a can of beer between the legs of a guy. So ladylike and so classy!

My travelling mate entered my name in the competition; I did not have a clue. After a few drinks, it was my turn. It was funny. It was easy to run towards the target, but the return was unpredictable. After a couple of rounds, it was the final; I started to get good at it, and was able to control the situation. I did master to manage the return; I put all my weight and my strength to make sure I was not flying backwards. I wanted to win this prize. I put my knees on the floor, and got carpet burn, but went on to win. It was a cruise on the Great Barrier Reef, with an introduction to diving, bungee jumping, and a day of water rafting.

I was very excited at another opportunity to explore Australia. I called mum and dad and told them I had won the prize. They were not very impressed, especially me going bungee jumping; another one of my crazy moments.

During my bungee jumping trip, I met two nurses from Melbourne. They were staying at Port Douglas, at the Sheraton; a beautiful, magical hotel. They had two massive bedrooms. I was complaining about my ten beds backpackers' room, not being able to relax in the shower, or dropping my clothes on the floor and always getting them wet. Poor little me, having to travel around Australia and still complaining! They suggested I stay in one of their rooms for one night. That was so kind of them. They were so lovely. It was just beautiful. By the way, I did jump, but they did not.

I also went to Cape Tribulations for a couple of days, where the rainforest meets the sea. Once again, it was enchanting. The public phone was solar operated; there was no electricity and we could not just make a phone call whenever we felt like it. We saw a crocodile on the beach. We could not swim because it was jellyfish season; we went canoeing to the Cape, wearing stockings. I was living the exciting and adventurous life of a backpacker; it was fun. I briefly went to Brisbane, and then back to Sydney. This was my first trip around Australia.

Upon returning to Sydney, Shane was opening a new office in Newcastle. I went there too. I was living with the team, and then later with Michelle. I was so fortunate, as she took me under her wing. I travelled everywhere; bushwalking and boating on Lake Macquarie. She had a passionate life and was such a positive soul. I met her 30 years ago. She understood life back then. I was still going about my own business, without knowing what the world had in store for me.

I finally left to go back to France via Perth. After nine months in Australia, it was time for me to go back and finish my third year. I left Perth in February, during summer and arrived in Paris in winter. I was freezing cold. I could not speak French properly; I was stumbling on the words. I was finally fluent in English; my English teacher was impressed. I submitted my end of third year report, and was awarded a distinction.

October 1992. The Return to Australia.

Shane - Sydney

I decided to go back to Australia, and not finish my fourth year at university. It was a big disappointment for my father. But I had to go back; I was in love with Shane. I will explain the details of my love story in another chapter. Back to Sydney in October 1992, Shane and I travelled extensively. I was not allowed to work at the time because of the visa conditions. As soon as I had the green light to start working again, I was hired by a marketing company, a Telco company, Australian Power. I resigned from Australian Power when I was pregnant. Shane was extremely focused on his goal; and he did achieve a lot for himself.

In 1995, we celebrated Shane's 30th birthday. I had organised a surprise party on the Yarra River, and it was great. I was pregnant, and I was not feeling too well on the boat. All the Black Magnets came. It was a great surprise party.

We were a couple, a soon-to-be family, and we spent Christmas at his parents' at Shepparton. We attended several weddings from the Black Magnets, his school friends. Thanks to Victoria, I still hear about them from time to time. They have always made me feel special, welcoming me into their circle. I would like to take this opportunity to say thank you to all of them. Shane's friends, the Black Magnets, are great people, and I still treasure the memories we have together.

I was, once again, living a very privileged life. We travelled a lot. We went skiing and jet skiing at Lake Eildon, and spent time in Queensland with Gary and Cyndi, Shane's longtime friends. They used to come down to ours and we used to go up to theirs. They loved playing cricket for hours in their backyard. For an awfully long time, they did not grow up. Their friendship was and still is beautiful.

Once, for my birthday, Shane hired a boat as a present, and twelve of us went sailing on the Sydney Harbour. He was well known for misplacing his keys or his wallet. I have always received the most luxurious gifts. He was and is still very generous. My friend Laure visited me when I was pregnant. We went to Brisbane, and with Cyndi, we went to Fraser Island; we were the three naughty girls at the back of the bus. After my friend's visit, Eric, my brother, also came down for Christmas. I met him in Cairns and Shane organised a three-day cruise on the Great Barrier Reef for my brother and I. I was huge and at six-and-a-half months pregnant, I could not go diving. Sleeping in a cabin was very tight, but I wanted to impress my big brother. We were creating great memories; jumping into the water and taking a tiny boat to go towards the reef. It was fun. But I could not go back inside the dingy because of my tummy. I took a rope, and they dragged me slowly back to the boat. Nothing or nobody was stopping me. We flew back to Sydney and left to drive to Melbourne. By this time, I was not authorised to fly anymore. It was a very memorable holiday.

While working at Australian Power, I met a terrific friend, Violaine. The first time we met in person was in the Rocks. I was expecting her to have a French accent, but it turned out I did not understand anything of what she was saying. She had an Irish accent. It took me a while to get used to it. I already had a problem understanding English, and was still getting used to the Australian accent. To now add the Irish one on top was pushing it a bit too much for me, to be honest. But my friendship with her was quite an adventure! Thanks to Violaine, I discovered a bit of myself; I started to enjoy reading, and my favourite books are from Sinead Moriarty, her close friend from Ireland. She is so inspiring. I wanted her to tell my story, I wanted her to make you laugh, but this is my journey and I had to do it with my talent and my beautiful flaws. I also discovered my passion for musicals, thanks to Violaine. She has been here for me for the whole duration of my relationships, without judgement; just with love and complete acceptance.

I also remember Debbie and Edwyrd. When I had Victoria, she had Huw, an impossible name for me to pronounce. We are still in touch, and she resides on the other side of Australia.

My parents visited in May, accompanied by my 81-year-old grandma. I weighed just over 67 kilograms. We took my grandma everywhere: Teppanyaki restaurant, cruising on Sydney Harbour for Mother's Day, Blue Mountain, and the first live play of "The Phantom of the Opera." Victoria, my two months old baby, was with us and we had to buy her a full-price ticket.

It was a memorable holiday. During this trip, my father asked Shane if he was going to marry me one day. I did not remember his answer, but my parents did: "No, she is too short." Was that a joke or was he serious? Regardless, we never got married.

Shane and I separated in August 1996; Victoria was 6 months old. He had given me two beautiful gifts; the first one was my daughter, and the second one my dog, DeeDee, my German Shepherd. I had her for ten years. She went for six months to Shepparton, where Shane's parents looked after her. When Victoria and I moved to Brisbane, she moved in with us. DeeDee travelled with me to South America, we had a stopover in Paris, stayed in Reims at my parents' place, and finally arrived in French Guinea in South America. She came back and stayed four weeks in quarantine, and flew back to Brisbane. She died at the age of 10 from cancer. I had to put her down, and it was very sad. I know some people will not understand why I was so attached to my dog; but they just become a part of the family. I have and will always treat them as such. My life in Australia has always been about following my heart. It is hard to separate my lovers from my work experience. I am not a career woman; my priority is my children. Nevertheless, I did not enjoy to just be a stay at home mum; I wanted to achieve more, but I thought I had to copy my mother in order to give Victoria the best opportunities in life.

I went back to France in October 1996, and I only weighed 39 kilograms. I was too skinny. I was pretending it was due to breastfeeding, but I was heartbroken. The only person who knew

Virginie

that Shane and I were separated was Eric. My mum found me unpleasant with Shane. She could not understand why. Mum and dad had finally retired, and they had organised for the whole family to spend Christmas together in a ski resort. It had been 12 years since our last Christmas together, and all my brothers and sister were there with their spouses and their kids. Shane agreed to play the game and not say anything. I told him: "I'm not going to spoil their holidays because we are separated." I did not tell anyone else, except my older brother, Eric. I was supposed to pick Shane up from the airport and wanted to go to Violaine's wedding in Paris. But it was not possible. Mum and dad wanted everybody there. And I owed them to, at least, respect their wishes.

When we settled in the Chalet, Eric suggested to go out. Shane was tired, and he stayed with Victoria. I went out with my brother. He saved me; I was so sad, but I had to pretend everything was fine. I did not want to spoil anyone's holidays. Shane and I were courteous to each other, and we pretended we were still ok. On the last day skiing, Eric, who is an excellent skier, challenged Shane, who also happened to have the same skills, to jump off some random hills. Shane fell off and dislocated his shoulder. Was it revenge from my brother? Or maybe Karma? We will never really know.

After the holidays, Shane and I flew to London for his work. I stayed back in London while he travelled through England. At the hotel, I met one of my old friends from Business School. She upgraded me to a suite with Victoria and we spent some evenings together. Shane thought I had upgraded myself as a revenge, to make him pay, but it was only a gift from my friend. I never really thought about revenge.

We went back to Sydney, where I packed Victoria's stuff: 12 boxes of toys and her cot. I only took my futon bed, two boxes of belongings and my suitcase. During the separation process, Shane was incredibly supportive. Overwhelming feelings of guilt or generosity? Probably both.

Now when I think about it, I was not happy at the time. I thought I was happy, but did I even know what made me happy? Shane and I had stayed together for five years.

The Move to Brisbane, January 1997.

I arrived in Brisbane, where I stayed with Cyndi and Gary. They protected me; they cherished me and helped me settle in my new home, until I was able to get back on my feet. They introduced me to Queensland life.

It was then that I realised I could not do anything on my own. I had never made enough money, I was not independent, I did not have a permanent visa, I was still in a de facto relationship, and I was trapped. Fortunately, our priority with Shane had always been Victoria. We managed to settle everything without a lawyer. Trust me, it was not all smooth; I was angry with him, and I was very hurt.

4th of July 1997.

With Shane's help, I bought a house on Elfreda Street, and we moved in with our dog DeeDee. It was a happy place. It was my home, and this is where Victoria grew up.

It was there that I built my French network, a community of beautiful people. I met extraordinary friends, who have been here for me through thick and thin for the past 30 years. Rosa and Ly Fu, Lydie and Jason, Christine and Keith, Dominique and Karine, Laurel and Michel, Blandine and Pierce, Mathias and Jane, Sylviane and Ian, Pascale and Danny, and David and Rebecca; it is important for me to mention their names, as they are still so dear to my heart to this day.

This was my family. I did not have anyone else here. We were living close to Rosa; my "adoptive" sister. My heart had chosen her; she was so similar to my own sister. We shared the same values, but we did not have anything else in common. She loved reading and I did not. The choice of our movies was always challenging. I love sports, she does not, but I respect and love her and her family as my own. She has been through my highs and lows, always there.

Within a year, I did some renovations: new kitchen, new bathroom. I remember moving to this house and on the first night, while opening the cupboards, it felt to me like a million small cockroaches had just been dumped on the floor. I was shocked; what kind of house did I buy? It was so scary that I cried. Oh my God! I imagined myself being one of the three little pigs, living in a house in the woods, scared that the big bad wolf would destroy it. Great memories in Elfreda Street!

It was a happy house; "La Maison du Bonheur," a house full of laughter and happiness.

The Consulate Years.

I managed to find some work. For over two years, I worked at the French Honorary Consulate, on a part-time basis. My priority was Victoria; she was going to a Montessori school 16 kilometres away from Alderley. I was always running late, and she often had breakfast in the car. I was always finishing dressing her up upon arriving at the school. My daughter had two best friends there, Lucy and Phoebe. Her favourite activity was to make butter and "Vegemite" crackers. I could not bring myself to eat "Vegemite" for seven years, but one of the promises I made to Shane was to make sure Victoria's tastebuds were exposed to it. I did such a good job that I now love it and my parents too. I regularly bring it to them when I go back home to France. Regarding Victoria's tastebuds, I still remember her going over to BJ and Charles', Phoebe's parents, for a sleepover. One day, she was hungry and BJ gave her some cheese. It was Coon cheese, and my daughter scrunched up her nose and said: "That's not cheese, that's plastic!" To this day, we still laugh with BJ and Charles about it.

I have always had an entrepreneur spirit, and had been creating micro-enterprises on the side for a while. I still had a lot of ideas, I could not stand still. Since 1998, I had my own bookkeeping business, which allowed me to accommodate both Victoria's and my own needs. I did apply for a position to work FIFO to New Caledonia in 1998, but what was I thinking? I could not go; I was a single mum. But I never stopped believing in my dreams, hoping they would, one day, come to fruition.

The Consulate life was fascinating. From organising cocktails to helping French natives register their weddings, their nationality, the birth of their children, their passports, and their certificate of life for their pension in France, not one single day was exactly the same. I met Ambassadors, Consuls, Mayors, Senators; so many exciting and fascinating people.

Rosa and I met a French Senator, Mr Ferrand with Mr and Mrs Lejeune. He asked us why we had not yet established a French School. At the time, we had at least three students; Hugo and William, who were Ly and Rosa's kids, and Victoria. We finally did it, and "Les Petits Princes" was born. She was the mastermind and I was the talker. We were a great team.

I am the social butterfly; she is much more reserved than me. We somehow complemented each other. We used to spend all our weekends together. We were going from Sunshine beach with Dada and Rebecca plus "Les Nanas" (The Girls) to Byron Bay. We spent our weekends cooking nems, having BBQs, playing tennis, going to the beach and to the restaurant. I miss our weekends away.

Australia and Work Experience

When I left to go to South America, Matthias took over with Rosa. "Les Petits Princes" still exists today, and has grown even more beautifully.

In August 1997, Emmanuel and his wife Katia came to visit me with Jules, their son. We spent some beautiful evenings together. On the first night, we went to South Bank to a Greek restaurant, "Smashing Plate." Of course, my brother could not resist jumping in the South Bank water; I knew it was forbidden, but on top of that, he went skinny dipping. I had to explain to the police that they had just arrived, and we were celebrating; we were having too much fun. Shane had organised a lot of trips around Australia; three days at Magnetic Island, going diving and swimming with the stingrays.

We were supposed to go to Sydney and I had planned to stay with Debbie, who just had twins. They were sick, and our plan had changed. I called Shane to ask if I could stay at his place, but someone had already replaced me in the family home. I was so upset that I refused to go. I let my brother, his family and Victoria go by themselves. I did not know, but Shane had organised accommodation for everybody. I was hurt, again. Their trip to Sydney was memorable, as Shane knows how to entertain his guests. Before they went back to France, Shane took us to Noosa. While having dinner, my family was commenting on how wonderful Shane was, and he really was, except for the fact that he had broken my heart and I was still sad. But as usual, I pretended to be happy, just to please everybody.

1998.

I was still working for the French Honorary Consulate in Brisbane I received a phone call from Julie. She was enquiring about whether

Virginie

I knew of anyone who could help them practice their French, as their daughter Mikki was in France on an exchange program for one year. Of course, with my big heart, I offered my services. When Mikki came back, she did not want to go back to boarding school. They asked me if I could accommodate her while they were overseas. She was in year 12 and had her own car. She was 17, and exactly like one of my daughters today. Mikki was fun, and was taking care of Victoria as if she was her big sister. As soon as I was gone, the music would be on full blast at home, with a two-year-old girl dancing on the table, as her mother would, singing "I feel like a woman." I thought it was ridiculously cute.

By writing this book, I had to go down memory lane. The cover photo of this book is from the Sunshine Coast. When my parents visited, they used to stay at Rebecca and David's, on the Sunshine Beach. We have collective fond memories of this place. After 17 years, while in the Sunshine Coast with Jill, I met Julie and Cavan again. When I asked my daughter to look for accommodation to spend a couple of days together, she booked the exact same place that we used to go to with my parents, 16 years ago. It felt like life had come to a full circle; I was going back to basics, rediscovering the places I liked, and doing what I enjoyed doing, with the people I love.

September 1999.

One of my most memorable encounters. I nicknamed him "The Pirate." He had arrived from New Caledonia with his boat, and had a visa. But he also had a passenger, who had forgotten to apply for a visa. He was fined $5,000 for failing to comply with legislation. I helped him write a letter to apologise to the authorities. He had travelled the world; I was the only one from the Consulate who ever bothered to try to help. He was impressed, and I gained a friend for life. Until this day, I can always count on my pirate. He arrived the week of my 30th birthday. It was a fancy dress-up party. We had pirates, gypsies, angels, nuns and convicts. It was a great night.

2000.

I went to France for three months to celebrate my parents' 40 years wedding anniversary.

When Mikki left to go back to France, she fell in love, and married a French man. We lost touch with each other, but while writing this book, I did some research and found her on Facebook. We have since reconnected. I am still in Australia, and she is still in France. Her parents now live on the Sunshine Beach, and we have also reconnected.

My passion was not my career; my priority has always been the kids. I will explain this in more details in the chapter about motherhood. I worked many casual jobs; I had my own bookkeeping company for quite a while. Later on, in life, it was time to concentrate on my career. I did work in the mining industry; it was a dream when I arrived in Brisbane, to work between New Caledonia and Australia. I had the best of both worlds; friends, Karen and Xavier, the French culture, food, and shopping. I had always wanted to travel. Back in 1998, I applied for a job, but because I was a single mum with no family support, I could not go just yet. You do not know when you will achieve your dreams, but if you keep believing in them, they will end up happening, sooner or later.

Twenty years later, I finally reached my goal to go to New-Caledonia for work. I was working in human resources and finance. New Caledonia meant a lot to me; I could catch up with Karen and Xavier, but also with my friend "the Pirate."

I was passionate about this job. I probably worked too hard. Around this time, I met my adoptive brother, Casimir. He was always supportive, just like Rosa. My heart had adopted both; to me, they are family and to this day, they are still here for me. My job was fascinating; I was in charge of the contracts for the Australians working in New Caledonia. I was the link between the French and the Australians. I could speak French and English; I was dealing with all sorts of people, ranging from foremen, truck drivers, administration staff, engineers, and managers. I loved the responsibility of being the intermediary, relaying important information to the two cultures. I put myself through a lot of stress, but it was fun. I have positive memories working for this company. Casimir is terribly similar to Eric, my brother and he was born on the same day as Jill's father; it was not a good omen, but definitely not his fault. I met his family and his sisters in Brisbane. His wife Anne-So welcomed me as a part of the family. They got married in Japan; they are such an inspiration. Anne-So is now the vice president of "Les Petits Princes." What a small world!

I also met Sam or Samantha, who now lives in New Zealand; we worked together, and we laughed together. She just seems to understand me so easily. We did catch up for a weekend in Sydney, and we had so much fun going to the movies in a gold class cinema. We were in bed by 9 pm every night; we were so exhausted! She, and her family, have always been very inspiring. They follow their dreams, and they are true to themselves.

Australia and Work Experience

Since then, I did recover physically from cancer. The emergence of cancer in my body acted as a catalyst; it was my body giving me a clear warning. What was going to follow would change my life, forever.

I was back to work full-time, this time with a French company. I was feeling incredible; it was fun to share the French culture. My manager was young and generous. After 18 months, I could not pretend anymore. I was back at the same crazy schedule that I had put myself through; stress, long hours, blaming everybody else for my inability to say no. It started to eat me from the inside. I was feeling guilty about work and my family. Out of the blue, I had to stop; my tank was empty. The French company kindly accepted to let me go; they understood I had to take care of myself and my family. I can never thank them enough, but I will in the future. I spent 50 years becoming who I am today. 2019 was my reset year.

Chapter 4

My Lovers

I have always been friendly, helpful, have always needed cuddles, attention, and I am demanding; isn't every woman the same? I dedicate this chapter to my dad and to the fathers of my children; husbands, partners, lovers. This is not a judgement; it will be a mea culpa. I am ready to accept my faults. This chapter was not easy to put together; it was an eye opener and quite confronting for me to relive these memories, to be honest. I hope you will enjoy the read.

My first boyfriend was not a boyfriend as such, but just a boy. I got teased by my siblings because I liked him. I never kissed him; his name was Willy. At the time, I was a fan of the cartoon "Maya the Bee." They used to call me Maya, and I was always so embarrassed.

I had my first French kiss when I was 13 years old; I was so disgusted that I did not kiss anyone else until I was 17 years old.

1986.

My first serious boyfriend was **Frédéric** and he was a gymnast. All my friends were in Year 12, and I was still in Year 10 but living alone, compared to them who were still living with their parents. I still practiced fencing three or four times a week, plus competition. I had good results enough to qualify for the interregional and the national championship. I had a studio, and life was more complicated living on my own; I needed to feed myself, do shopping and study. Always be wary of what you wish for. I worked very hard, and partied equally hard. We were going to the "Metro," a nightclub in Nancy. I was always scared to meet my brother there. After partying, we were going back to my apartment at 6 am for breakfast. After our meal, they would drop me back at school at 8 am, where I had 2 hours of maths to start the day. I often had to go see the headmaster to be allowed to skip the 2 hours of sport between 10 and 12 am. I was so tired. My name was in the local newspaper for my fencing results. She knew I was training hard; she probably did not think I was partying as hard. At 10 am, my friend and I would go back to my place to sleep. On Saturday night, I was usually invited by my friend's parents, and now that I think about it, this was probably the only decent meal of my week. Usually, Sunday was an all-day fencing competition. While I was away at home for the Christmas holidays, Frederic kissed another girl on New Year's Eve. I did not forgive him, and broke up. Last time I heard about him, he was a firefighter in Paris.

Summer 1987.

My parents had employed a new waiter, **Hervé**. I fell in love with him. Or, to be more precise, I thought I was in love with him. You must understand that, by this point, my world was upside down; I had lost my bearings. We had just moved to this town and I was not feeling great. I was just craving my parents' attention. My dad liked him very much; I believed I would have their approval. I wanted them to love and be proud of me. What I did not understand was that Hervé was still in love with Emmanuelle, his ex from another town, where he was living before accepting a new job offer. His passion was soccer.

I hope, dear reader, that you have watched the movie "Mamma Mia." I will use the dot, dot, dot expression to refer to you know what. So anyway, dot dot dot… I did it for the first time. He did not believe me. I should have known better. Like Princess Diana, I was not too fond of a "ménage à trois." I did not feel right. As a good Catholic, I thought I had to stay with him because I had slept with him. I felt increasingly trapped and disappointed. Dad told me that if I was not happy with him, I could still break up because we were not yet married. Very shortly after that, we separated.

For my 18th birthday party, I organised a big event. On top of my parents' bar, there was a ballroom where we had a massive party. My ex Frédéric, my current boyfriend Hervé, and my future boyfriend, Nicolas were all present.

1988, Year 12.

I fell in Love with **Nounours, while** he was in year 11. I was two years older than him, and his parents disapproved of the relationship. I was too old to be in grade 12, it seems. Why judge the book by its cover? We went to England together; his family is from Les Vosges, in the east of France. After the first meeting, his parents embraced me and treated me beautifully.

Virginie

In **February 1992,** when I came back from Australia, I told him I had been unfaithful with Shane, but we still stayed together. I went to New York for a work conference with S&G in July, and he left for work in Canada. I broke up with him while he was overseas. I broke his heart. We had an apartment together; I went back to Australia before his return, and my parents had to move my stuff out. I did put them in a bad situation; Nounours loved my parents and spent a lot of time with them when I was in Australia, instead of being with his own parents. I never saw him again. Years later, as I was in France with Victoria for Laure's wedding, he came to visit my parents at the farm, and he saw Victoria. He called me to see if I wanted to catch up, but I declined the invitation. Back then, I was single again as Shane had left me. Although Nounours had forgiven me for my betrayal, I could not go back to him. I thought that if I did what I did, it was not real love. I was still looking for the one.

I had a fling in Paris with **Jean-Marc.** We were colleagues, and after my trip to the US in **July 1992**, Shane asked me to come back to Australia to be with him. I was excited, but I could not trust him. My heart wanted to believe him, but my mind was telling me the opposite. I decided to leave France after the end of my third year of studies. I still had one more year to go, but I could not wait to run away, again.

Before I left to go back to Australia, I had a second thought: what if Jean-Marc was the one?

We spent some time together, and dot, dot, dot… My parents received my bank statement and were horrified that I had spent so much money for a weekend in the west of France, at Le Mont St Michel. To this date, it is still my favourite place. He was fun, he was in love with me, but I was in love with Shane. Things were progressing well with Jean-Marc. I told him I should stay here with him, but he encouraged me to go and see what would happen. He did not want me to doubt my choices. I needed to close the chapter with Shane.

Did he still want me? Did he love me? I was supposed to go for three months, from October to December. I worked in Paris, paid my rent for three months, saved some money and left.

When I arrived, Shane was with Nathalie, a colleague of mine. They were living together; he was sharing his accommodation, and there were always a lot of people around. Shane was not emotionally available, so I decided to go back to France. It was not what I had expected.

My God: expectations! They never stop.

Shane and I talked a lot; I remember looking at Coogee Beach and telling him clearly what I wanted, and what were my expectations. The little voice inside my head was telling me to go back; my heart was telling me to stay. After my conversation with Shane, I decided to leave. I tried to avoid him as much as possible. I did not want to see him, as I knew he would try to persuade me to stay.

I called Jean-Marc and my parents to let them know that I was coming back. They were so excited. I left for the airport. I checked in my luggage and went to customs. I was leaving, and Shane's chapter was closed.

But no! Here he was, at customs, asking me to stay. If I did love him, I should stay, shouldn't I? It was so romantic!

Virginie

I said yes. I was happy.

We needed to get my suitcase back, telling the airline I could not leave and requesting to get my bag out of the plane. I had to explain that I had changed my mind. I was in love.

I never used to be jealous, but when I was with him, I was unable to trust him regarding women. I could trust him with everything else. He is an excessively kind and beautiful person, and we share the same family values. But our values regarding romantic relationships differ considerably.

I had to make two difficult phone calls: the first one to Jean-Marc, and the second one to my parents.

A few years later, I went to see Jean-Marc, and we went to our favourite restaurant in Paris. The owner recognised us, and called us his love birds. It was a bit awkward. We talked and we knew we would be ok. What I did find out two years later was that Jean-Marc was so excited that I was coming for Christmas, that he wanted to propose. I was surprised, but I guess it was not meant to be.

In December 1992, Shane and I moved in together. I only had one request: to be together. We always had guests staying with us; some were staying for a short term, some for a longer period. In principle, I did not mind; I had always been a social butterfly. But I wanted him for myself; his business was based on relationship building. I know it sounds selfish, but I felt so insecure. I was utterly dependent on him. No visa, no work, no money, no airfare to go back. I had lost my return ticket. I had put myself in this situation, I had chosen it, and I was too proud to ask my parents for money. I felt trapped, and unable to express myself clearly to Shane.

My Lovers

I tried to find my happiness, but I was unable to. I used to believe that if he was not close to me, I could not be happy. But I was suffocating him. I changed from being an adventurous, independent young woman to trying to be the perfect housewife. I put so much pressure on myself. I supposed I wanted to be like my parents, and I forgot who I was and what I wanted to achieve for myself. Our relationship fell apart, crippled by infidelity and insecurity, but our separation was a success.

Life with Shane was always so busy. We went to France to visit my parents; I remember going out in the streets of Paris with my brother Emmanuel, Katia and Shane, looking for a kebab at 5 am. I told him we could found croissants but no kebabs, unfortunately.

Every year, the Black Magnets attended the Grand Prix, wearing their uniforms. One year, I packed a survival backpack for their trip: Panadol, Berroca, lollies, bubble gums, spare socks, and undies. Their yearly trip was special for me; this is where Shane and I kissed for the first time.

In **1996**, after the birth of Victoria, we separated, and I moved to Queensland with Cyndi and Gary. I went back to France in October 1996. Shane joined my family for the Christmas celebration in France, and we pretended we were still ok. We had our ups and downs, and when the anger was gone, we could communicate beautifully. I was still looking for happiness.

I will not give details of the flings that I had; the one night stands or the weekend affairs. But I need to set the record straight for my dad: I have never been with a married man, never been out with my friends' exes, and I have never dated any of my friends; Vincent, Didier and Jean-Baptiste were just friends. They were my musketeers from the time I was fencing in my hometown.

Virginie

I have never really felt beautiful; it was always a point of conversation with my sister and my mum. I thought I was the ugly little duck, and my sibling was so beautiful. Was I the postman's daughter? (Sorry mum and dad, that's a joke!) But I guess it is just my perception, as we are in fact very similar.

I met a New-Zealander through Gary and Cyndi; he was beautiful, a gentleman, hardworking, an excellent father. He had a daughter who was about the same age as Victoria. I was not patient with her. I was selfish; it was already hard for me to be a single mum. He was going through a nasty separation. I could not deal with his issues. We could be a team, but I was scared. He needed to protect his daughter, and I needed to save mine. I did not have the strength to be with him. The time we had together was fun and full of tranquility, but I was not ready. Is it what you called the rebound? We went to visit his parents in New Zealand for his birthday; we could not share the same room, it was a feeling of déjà-vu; our parents shared the same values. I wanted more, but I did not know what. I was still so hurt.

Another episode that I must relate is about a colleague, who became what I thought was an excellent friend. We were both separated. Without warning, one afternoon, he arrived at my house with a big bunch of red roses, champagne, and a ring, exactly as in a fairy tale. The only problem was that I did not love him. He had two kids, and even if we had spent a lot of time together, we were not involved romantically. He went to France to ask my hand to my father, and if I remember correctly, my dad said: *"He could not give my hand to him as it was mine to give, and I had been doing my own thing for a very long time."* Another memorable event that I had imposed on my parents. Poor them! They could not speak English, he could not speak French and he had arrived one hour earlier. It was a disaster. Anyway, I set

My Lovers

some rules, the first one being that he would not move in with me, and I would not babysit his kids. But each time, he insisted. I did not like the persistence and as I was not in love with him, I did not want to please him. I refused to be a co-dependant. Two weeks after the engagement party, I split up with him. It was a disastrous relationship, but a great party.

I went on a quest, as I wanted to be married by the age of 30, in **1999**. I was tired of receiving proposals from married men and losers who just wanted to move in with me. One of the first questions I asked most people I met was whether or not they were ready to marry me. I can't imagine how scary that attitude would have been for any potential date. While I was working at the Consulate, a gentleman called Christopher told me: "I'll give you my passport for a French Visa, and you give me your heart." He was as blunt as I was, and I liked it. I said we could start at lunch. We had a lot of things in common, but I was not ready for dot, dot, dot. He had offered to drop me off at home, but my car was parked at the train station, and we agreed that he would drop me off at my car. He tried for a kiss. I just smiled, and left. The next day, I received a huge bunch of flowers. He was on his way; I called a friend of mine, as I did not want to be alone with him. I was busy with Victoria, and I left him with my friend. Years later, we had dinner together, and we talked about that evening. He told me that nobody had ever pushed him in someone else's arms the way I did. I was married, and he smiled, saying that I knew precisely what I wanted: to be married. And he was right. I was.

My number one criteria regarding the person I intended to marry: someone with no kids. I did not want any baggage; I had heard many horror stories. He should also know how to dance (since I absolutely love dancing), must be courageous, and have a job.

Virginie

I made a promise to Shane: to not take Victoria away from him, so he could always have a relationship with his daughter.

I went to France for three months in 2000, for my parents 40th wedding anniversary. I enrolled Victoria in a French School, as I wanted her to be fluent in French and exposed to the language. I also went skiing with my brother. Serge was a friend of my older brother. They did compulsory army together. I was babysitting Eric's kids when they were going out. He was nine years older than me. My brother had a lot of respect for him. After skiing, I did my tour of France, visiting my friends. Serge invited me to see him too, and we started a relationship. I went back to Australia at the end of June 2000. He came to visit in October, and we got married the same year.

I did not tell my parents. My dad wrote in his book:

> *"One day, I told her that I was fed up with receiving my future ex-sons-in-law, and I no longer wanted to make sentimental investments. I was in constant heartache, and the next one had to be the right one. We were shocked when we were introduced to Serge, whom she had espoused in Australia without notifying her parents."*

I always had a provocative attitude, calling "a cat a cat" or as you say in Australia "a spade a spade." I could not bring any man at home if I did not have a ring on my finger, even when Shane came to France. They put us in a hotel. I thought it was silly, as we were already living together in Australia. But my parents wanted to make a point.

When I informed my parents that I was coming back for Christmas, and that I intended to go to French Guyana with Serge, my father started talking about sleeping arrangements;

My Lovers

I could not expect to share the same bed as Serge. As usual, I was not happy, and my hot temper and impulsiveness led me to prepare my vengeance. We went for dinner, and I explained to dad that, regarding the sleeping arrangement tonight, I had found the perfect solution. I was now a married woman, and this was my husband. It was not nice at all, to just blurt it out over dinner. Mum was upset, dad was not surprised. I am impulsive, stubborn, and I suppose I have inherited these traits from dad. As the saying goes: "The apple does not fall far from the tree." Serge and I lived in Kourou, in French Guiana. The lifestyle was better compared to France, but the standard of living was not comparable to Australia. I found it unsafe and violent. My work at the Space Centre was fun and exciting; the "Optus" satellite was launched from there. It was a great experience. If you read the book "Papillon," you will know where we were living. Closer to the Amazon sediments, the beaches were brown, but further towards the islands, it was a beautiful blue sea, but also full of sharks.

Life in French Guiana was tranquil, but Victoria was quite sick with staphylo. She was having way too many antibiotics, and her red blood count was low. For two weeks, I had to keep her at home, as her whole body was covered with sores. The climate was so humid that she could not heal outside. Overall, it was a good experience. I am glad I did it. I met Beatrice, a very close friend, and I learnt a lot from her, both personally and professionally. She was a significant encounter in the start of my awareness journey. I became a beautician, as I wanted to open a Beauty Salon in Brisbane.

In August **2001**, Serge and I got married in France. At the time, my grandma France was sick. She was living by herself until June 2001, when she had a fall and had to move in with my parents.

Virginie

She started using a stick first, then a walker, and by August, she attended the wedding in a wheelchair. We were concerned for her, but she stayed for the whole duration of the wedding, and asked me why I was getting married to Serge. She thought that we were not a good match; according to her wisdom, I was the Hare, and he was the Tortoise. It was nonetheless a great wedding, thanks to my parents who had organised everything. I felt a bit like a spectator; I had been living in Australia for the past ten years, and there was only one guest from Down Under: Therese and her daughter, who were nannying in Switzerland. My parents had invited all our relatives, and Serge had invited his family and friends. My oldest friend Laure was there too; our friendship is such that I can go for ten years without seeing her, but we are always present for each other, and each time we reunite, it feels like we had parted ways just yesterday.

My grandma passed away a couple of weeks later; I could not go to the funeral as the air controllers in France were on strike, again. It was tough to grieve by myself, as we had been very close. She used to come to Paris and I would then tell her my stories. I knew she would repeat everything to mum, and that was a way for mum to know everything without me having to say anything. That's the beauty of having grandparents or a very tight-knit community to rely on.

After the wedding, I fell pregnant, and was also diagnosed with dengue fever. We spent Christmas in France, and in January, we went back to Australia. I miscarried on the plane, somewhere between Paris and Singapore. But as usual, I did not want to run late on our schedule, and we went on to catch our connection flight. It was then confirmed that I had lost the baby, but I had the all clear from the hospital to get back on my feet, and back to the original plan. We had planned to attend the Australian Open, and a romantic honeymoon. We caught up with friends, and went back to South America, and made preparations for our return to Australia. I was now officially a beautician.

But once again, I changed my mind, and wanted to try a different business venture; importing video vending machines with Serge. Being in 2020, you would be less accustomed to seeing DVD stores, but at the time, it was very different and people relied mainly on Blockbuster and Video Ezy stores for their "home movie fix." Maybe I was a bit too advanced for the market. I was also pregnant, and I wanted to give birth in Australia. I moved back just after Christmas.

January 2003.

I moved back to Elfreda Street. William, Rosa's son, came over to help me, and all my friends were there. I felt like a beached whale; a romantic expression taken from my dad. Serge reached Australia on time, and witnessed Jill's birth. Starting the business was not as easy as it had seemed. I had failed to plan that technology would be developing so quickly. Human beings were still being employed as car park ticket officers. I was ten years early. We did not want to give up yet; Serge and I worked in different jobs to be able to maintain the business and to keep paying the bills.

Serge did not wish to stay in Australia; he wanted to go back to France, and DeeDee had passed away. Life seemed hard. We had a roof over our heads, we were in good health; what else did we want?

Virginie

We then met my second future husband, who lived two blocks away from us. I had already met him in **1998** when he was still married. We went with "Les Nanas" to see Sylviane's husband, Ian, perform with his band. Ian was playing with my second husband's brother and sister in law. It was a dress-up party.

My second husband had two girls from a previous relationship; they used to come around the house to play with Victoria when Jill was still a baby.

While he was around, I tried to set him up with some friends, but he was not too keen to be with anyone at the time. We had dinner regularly with him at home on Wednesdays. I was then working, with my accountant, at his Strathpine office; we only had one car and a scooter. I was travelling to Strathpine every day, while Serge looked after the kids. My second husband offered to relocate the business in the spare room at his place, which was two blocks away. It was very tempting to not have to drive this much, as the company was not doing that well. I think my second husband just wanted to be involved in the business. Shares were moved between Serge, the accountant, my second husband and I.

Serge wanted to go back to France; we were planning to go on a holiday for Christmas. For various reasons, I was increasingly frustrated with Serge, and he was probably also frustrated with me. I could sense he was unhappy. He had not completely resigned from his work back in France. He had taken a leave for two years, as he did not want to stay in Australia permanently. But I had made a promise to Shane; I assured him that I would not leave Australia until Victoria turned 16, and it was a part of the deal that I would not leave. I assumed that Serge was feeling trapped, stuck in a country that was not his own.

My Lovers

We had friends, a house, a business, and most importantly, we were healthy. We were not very successful with the vending machine business, but it had only been 18 months so far, and trial and error was always a part of the journey. Should we keep going, or should we stop? I wanted to keep going, and when I met my second husband, he said, resolutely: "Yes, we can make it work." Serge was okay with the idea.

Our trip to France was getting closer, and I tried to train my second husband to hold the business while we were away. Serge was going for four weeks with the kids, and I was going for two weeks. I asked Serge to organise the two weeks that we were supposed to spend together. I did not want to be spending the whole time catching up with people. I wanted us to go somewhere as a family with Victoria and Jill, like skiing. From my perspective, I was not asking for too much. I just wanted to go skiing, but nothing was organised. I was getting increasingly frustrated, and impatient. It felt to me that I was carrying the business on my own. Jill, who was one year old, and Victoria were playing in the street. I was overwhelmed with the work, doing everything; translating, paperwork, business, and on top of that, I tried my best to make my husband happy.

When a shoulder came for me to lean on, I did not hesitate a second; it turned out to be my second husband. I was very flattered that he liked me. We had just started working together. One night, during our Wednesday night dinner conversations, we were comparing our opinions about attractive women. Serge and my second husband happened to have the same taste, but I completely disagreed with them. I thought they were just judging on age, while overlooking style and look. After my second husband left, Serge told me he was concerned, as my second husband had the same taste as him. If that's the case, he thought, then he must find "my wife" beautiful. I dismissed what he was saying as nonsense. You can call me naive or an idiot, but on the next day I went and repeated this comment to my second husband. He told me it was true. I felt uneasy; I could not pursue a working relationship with him anymore, as I was uncomfortable. On the way to a meeting, my second husband kissed me. I was so confused.

My impulsive nature was taking over again, and I had another heated argument with Serge, during which I decided I was not going to France anymore. I told him I was tired of repeating the same things over again, to compromise all the time. And within a week, I told him that our marriage was over.

I left Serge, and moved in with my second husband. What was I thinking? Well, I was clearly not thinking, just acting impulsively, again.

What I did to Serge was unacceptable; I did not give him a single chance. It was over. I was not unhappy, but I was not happy. But what exactly was I looking for?

Serge and Jill spent their Christmas holidays with my parents. I think all my siblings and my parents were not impressed that he was still coming to theirs. I still do not know why he chose to be with my family instead of his own. He was a great dancer; he was also funny and prickly. I must admit that my grandma was right; we were indeed hugely different. I think we both wanted to be married. Perhaps we were both looking for emotional security. He ticked all the boxes, and he loved the fact that he was becoming a part of our family. He liked my brother so much. As for me, I always wanted to create a happy family, or maybe please everybody?

My Lovers

We ended up separating. Serge still intended to go to France with Jill for the holiday season. After working at the French Consulate for years, I was accustomed to the "Code Civil" (Civil Law), and I wanted Serge to sign specific paperwork to ensure they were coming back. He refused and asked "Les Nanas" to convince me. And I did listen to them. If only I had not! I was confused between listening to my guts and my impulse. With time, I should have tried to do things differently, but I did not. Unfortunately, I can't go back to the past, so I just have to use my experience as a lesson for the future.

The funny thing is that he did not go visit his family, while in France, but he stayed with mine. And I think my parents and my siblings just hated me for having to spend Christmas with my ex. I can only imagine how uncomfortable his company was, especially when he was repeating to my daughter that I had abandoned her. I suppose he was angry and sad. I was not as nice as he had thought; the way I had treated him was awful. Just imagine if someone did this to me? I would have felt so wronged. But of course, I was in my own little selfish bubble, and unable to acknowledge the collateral damage caused.

After those holidays, Serge came back to Australia. I rented a house for three months for him, until we could agree for settlement. That would give him time to decide what he wanted to do. I rented my house, and I moved in with my second husband. By then, I was pregnant. We decided that yes, we wanted a sibling for Jill. And I remember having a very specific request. I told him that: "I wanted two children from the same father." He promised that he would fulfil my demands.

My second husband had two girls, and I had two of my own; in total, we had four girls.

Virginie

Just after Jill's birthday, while Serge had weekend access to her, I started having an uncomfortable feeling. I went to his house and saw the lights on, but no car. I assumed he went to visit a friend. But I was still surprised though, because he always turned off the lights. I had this uneasy feeling the whole weekend. Was it my pregnant guts, or my maternal instincts and feelings kicking in?

On Sunday night, at five o'clock, I received a phone call from Serge. He told me they were back in France, and that I would not see my daughter again. I only remember the crushing feeling of my heart breaking. I fell on the floor, and screamed my soul out. It felt like my heart had just been pulled out of my chest. I was torn, ripped apart.

My second husband was a trained army officer; as soon as this happened, he turned on his survival mode. Off we went to the Australian Federal Police. This was now officially considered a kidnapping!

My second husband, while carrying out his work duties, had met a beautiful lady who had once experienced the same situation. She guided us through the process. We had to undergo the horrible procedures involved in the Hague Convention and the abductions of children.

I went to court, and saw a lawyer and a barrister. We needed a court order, which then had to be sent to the Federal Police, in Canberra. We were required to have all the paperwork translated to French, in order to be sent to the "Quay d'Orsay" (the French Ministry of Foreign Affairs) in France. It was a very stressful period. When we finished dealing with the lawyers in Brisbane, we then had to pass on the information to the lawyers in France;

it was a full-time, 24 hours job. During that time, we also had to take care of the other kids.

One thing was reassuring though; her safety was not compromised. I knew that Serge would take good care of her. But that was our life for six weeks, while I was pregnant. I am glad my second husband stopped me in my impulsiveness. I was ready to take the first plane out of Australia. And the outcome would have been hugely different.

The Tuesday following the abduction of my daughter, who was just two years and two weeks old, I received the divorce papers from France. What I did not know at the time was that, as soon as I were to set foot in the French territory, we would have been judged under the French divorce laws. If I was in France, I would not have been able to file a case for abduction. In France, you must appear in person in front of the judge for the divorce. You cannot be represented by a lawyer.

The court order needs to be translated before being sent to France. The whole process can take up to two years.

After a week, after putting through the application in Canberra, I asked: "How much longer will it take to send the paperwork to France?"

They replied: "We don't have any translator."

Fortunately, I was able to use my connections through the French Consulate. My networking came in handy, as I knew many French NAATI translators. I put the Embassy in contact with Annick, after calling her first. I had known Annick for a long time, through functions while I was working at the Honorary

French Consulate. I explained the situation, and asked her if I could refer her to Canberra to help them translate the documents related to my court case. I just wanted to know when it was done, so I could let my French lawyer know the progress. I added: "I know they've got it, and they just have to send it to France, so we can go ahead with it."

She translated everything, and called me back to say the paperwork was done. It took six weeks before I could go back to France as an Australian citizen. Six weeks is a record time. It can take up to two years. I was not going to wait two years. My daughter was only two years old.

I still cannot comprehend how you can use your child as a blackmail tool. I think it is the worst thing you can ever do. It's now a thing of the past, as I know that Serge was only very angry, and the abduction seemed to be the only solution at the time. He was deeply hurt.

When all the paperwork was completed after six weeks, I was authorised to go to France without jeopardising the case. We had a court date issued both for abduction and divorce. I was going back to France as an Australian citizen who was coming back to regain custody of her daughter. Upon arrival, I was travelling with an Australian passport; the customs asked me why I was not travelling on a French one. I was ready to explode; their overzealousness was highly frustrating. Why worry about my passport when they did not even do their job properly six weeks ago, and never asked the father of my child for his authorisation to travel alone with my daughter! I managed to contain myself, did not reply and moved on.

When I arrived in France, dad, who is a fantastic mediator, managed to persuade Serge to have Jill for the weekend. I had not seen my baby in six weeks. She came to the airport; I could see her through the glass. I will always remember her screaming when she saw me. The same daughter who was always so independent, not as affectionate as the others, and who, at only 11 months old, had refused my breast. She had wanted a bottle to hold in her hands, was ready to go explore the world. She did not like cuddles or kisses from a young age. But here she was, sticking to me like glue, and so clingy. She did not leave me the whole weekend. And I could not stop kissing her, could not stop cuddling her. I had missed her so much.

Sunday night was time to say goodbye, after a weekend of celebration. Jill had to go back with my older brother. It was part of the negotiation with Serge. I put her in the car, and she started screaming. We did not want to be apart anymore. It was horrible. We eventually won the court case; we had Jill back, and we flew back with Victoria, just in time before going past the authorised date to fly internationally, as I was pregnant with David.

I was upset with Serge, and for a very long time, I did not talk to him. The following year, we had a court order stipulating that, if he ever took Jill again without my authorisation, he would go straight to jail, in France or in Australia. Since then, Serge has been a regular visitor to Australia with his wife, and Jill regularly goes to France. The abduction episode is now a thing of the past. We had to prioritise Jill's wellbeing, and till now we still have our ups and downs, but our daughter is a beautiful young lady, finishing her studies, and with a very, very, strong personality. He was my first husband.

My second husband and I had a three months honeymoon, after which our life was a rollercoaster. I was coming back to Australia, pregnant, with my two girls.

Virginie

David arrived into the world at the end of September. We now had five kids at home: four girls, one boy, and life was fairly good. I was now a step mum; something I had never really planned, as I had enough on my plate with my own dilemma of exes. We went through many ups and downs, especially with our teenage girls. I remember being a kid, never wanting to have girls because I felt that my relationship with my mother had been so strained. To now be a mother and step mum to six girls and one boy was very challenging, but I did my best at the time.

Our life organisation was hectic; we tried to combine all the holidays to match those of Victoria's father, Shane, in Melbourne. Fortunately, he was always very accommodating. We tried to match Jill's holidays with her dad's in France, and finally, my second husband's daughters with their mother. Having Christmas together was challenging, but we did it.

We were doing it all; working, not working, renovating, working, renovating. For the last 15 years, we were always putting the kids first and us, as a couple, last.

When I was pregnant with Mia, my parents came to visit, and we decided to get married. I had just divorced Serge, and I already had two kids from my second husband. At some stage, I said: "Oh, see, maybe I should ask Serge to pay child maintenance for the last two kids, as I was not divorced yet. I was still married to him." This was my twisted sense of humour, and I thought it was funny, but of course I was the only one to think so.

We got married on the 31st of December 2007, at home. We had Mia's christening prior to the wedding. My brother, Eric, surprised me, and my parents were there too. As I am writing this book, my lovers chapter is over. I am in the process of separating

My Lovers

from my second husband. All I can say is that I am fifty years old, my body is bearing the scars of my life, but I am still standing strong. Maybe I was not made to be in a relationship. Perhaps I was meant to carry the burdens of my life alone.

I have enjoyed my lovers' presence in my life; I have loved them all. I wanted to thank them for helping me become who I am.

Maybe I was not destined to be married, or to share my life with someone else. Maybe I need to be single. Or maybe I need to start thinking more before committing to any form of engagement.

Well, I still believe in love, but I don't think I can be with anyone. My goal is to take care of my children; hopefully, I can teach them not to make the same mistakes.

Chapter 5

Motherhood

Motherhood, a word loaded with meaning. Are we ever ready to become mothers? I am a mother of five kids, and a stepmother of two. I had my first child when I was 26 years old, and this is considered quite late in my family. I have always felt a lot of pressure from my parents to become a mother.

As a child, I remember thinking I just wanted to be a mum of boys. My relationship with my mum was always conflictual. I realise now that any teenager, whether boy or girl, will face challenges in their relationship with their parents.

I remember going to a meeting at my first daughter's school. I did not know what to expect for my teenager when she started high school. And the only thing I remember from this two-hour meeting was: "Do not even try to reason or be logical with them. Their brain is still under construction, with a lot of unused neural connections."

Virginie

According to the "Raising Children" website:

> *"Children's brains undergo a massive growth spurt when they are very young. By the time they turn six, their brains are already about 90 to 95% of adult size. But the brain still needs a lot of remodelling before it can function as an adult brain.*
>
> *This brain remodelling happens intensively during adolescence, continuing into your child's mid-20s. The main change is that unused connections in the thinking and processing part of your child's brain (called the grey matter) are 'pruned' away. At the same time, other connections are strengthened. This is the brain's way of becoming more efficient, based on the "use it or lose it" principle."*

Victoria was a beautiful accident; she was not planned. I had an ulcer in my stomach, and the medications I had to take were cancelling the contraceptive effect of the tablets. I was sick throughout the first three months of the pregnancy. I remember going to the Hunter Valley with Violaine and Tony, my oldest friends in Australia. I was vomiting every morning, and I remember always thinking why I couldn't hold anything down as usual, or perhaps I had over drank the night before. But no, of course, my body was changing. I was craving vanilla milkshake, chips and gravy at 8 o'clock in the morning. I was vomiting three times on the way to work, spending my whole morning in the toilets, and was not very productive. 26 kilograms later, Victoria was born. She only weighed 2.6 kilograms at birth. My father used to call me "a little whale." Regarding the birth, I did not have a clue about what to expect; it just hit me in the face. I loved the prenatal appointments in Australia, and the relationship you build with nurses and midwives. I always compare it to the health system in France, which, for my liking, is over medicalised. Here, you have only one or two scans, and that's it.

Motherhood

The birth and the delivery, oh, my God! What an unbearable pain! The night before the birth, Shane and I went out for dinner, and I ate every single dish, plus Shane's pasta. When I arrived home, I felt sick. My contractions started at around 10 pm, and by 1 am, we called and went to the hospital. We said goodbye to our dog DeeDee; she was so gentle and beautiful. Before we left, Shane kept asking: "Where is my key? And my wallet?" I am glad he had his head screwed onto his shoulders, and he managed to find them. Shane was always very busy and a hard-working type of person; he is who he is now thanks to the sacrifices he has made throughout his life. We went to the Sydney Hospital, which was quite old at the time. I was not ready; I was only two centimetres dilated. It was going to be a long night. I remember having a shower. And I remember the pain. Yes, a lot of pain. My sister and sisters in law back in France tried their best to reassure me: "Just ask for an epidural, and you will be fine." As I said, the medical world between France and Australia is incredibly different. By 8 am, I asked for an epidural, but I had forgotten that I had injured my lower back while horse riding when I was a child. The anaesthetist could not put the needle in. He tried three times. Shane did not look confident at all when he was looking at the procedure. The epidural was more painful than the birth itself. Very quickly, the room was filled with doctors and nurses. They told me to push and to be quick because the baby was not responding. Victoria had her umbilical cord tied around her neck. When she was finally born, she had a worryingly low Apgar test. She finally cried; she was ok. She was born at 1.40 pm.

Her skin looked like a dead chicken's skin; when you pinched it, it stuck together. But it did not last long; she was beautiful. Shane went back to work. I was supposed to be discharged on a Sunday. Shane went to celebrate fatherhood on Saturday night.

Virginie

He was, after all, a dad. On Sunday morning, he had celebrated a bit too much. He was late to pick me up, trying to clean up the place before our return. Being late, he had also forgotten to install the car seat. Our beautiful friends, Jill and Mike, had organised a meal to be delivered at home. Shane did not have time to go shopping. He was so excited to be a dad. We still had to pick a name for her. But we disagreed. The only way we agreed to find a name: We had 5 pages printed with girls' names and when he went home, he had to highlight all the ones that he liked, and I did the same thing. He wanted to call her Kathleen, but I had difficulty pronouncing it. Now imagine my parents! We needed to find a name that was easy on the tongue, in any language. The only name in that category that we both loved was Victoria. Her middle names were Catherine, after my sister, and Christine from my sister in law. Victoria does possess her two beautiful aunties' qualities. And they, like us, are very proud of her.

We stayed in the hospital; I was lost, I was a mum, I had a million questions. It was hard to breastfeed, and the old trick of the frozen cabbage that you leave in the bra worked wonders. One day, I burped her, and there was blood. I was very scared, but then realised that it was not coming from her; it was my nipple. I expressed the milk, and Shane fed her with the bottle.

She was a great baby. Shane was an excellent father. He was working hard., and partying hard. During this time, we disconnected. I probably had the baby blues, but who knows. Very quickly after Victoria's birth, he started going out regularly. One night, he did not come back. So one day in August, I packed his bag, and he moved out.

I could not keep going like this. One day, I said: "If you love me, you should leave me." And he did.

Motherhood

Did I mean that? I do not know.

But we did not hurt each other. Well, we did, but we were civil with each other. We both had so many angry moments, but still respected each other.

When I arrived in France to visit mum and dad, I was very sad, and very skinny. I went from weighing 65 kilos when they had left me in May down to 39 kilograms, which was quite scary. Mum was shocked and asked: "What did you do to yourself to be so skinny?" Heartbroken I was, but I didn't tell her at the time. I told her it was the miracle of breastfeeding.

My parents organised a Christmas reunion in 1996. It had been 12 years since we had not spent Christmas together. Mum and dad got us all together, after their retirement. So I arrived with Victoria, not giving much news about Shane. My parents were surprised, and told me that I was being rude. But I did not want to be hasty and rush back to Australia. I did not want it to be the wrong decision, and refused to be influenced by people around me. I needed to follow my guts and my own choices and be responsible for it.

My parents always thought that my relationship with Victoria was not healthy. I breastfed her until she turned 18 months old, which is very unusual in France. We were too close, according to them. But is there such a thing as being too close to your own children, the ones you had carried inside you for nine months? A particular word became recurring: "fusional." That's how my parents would describe my relationship with my daughter. I realised now that this was how my parents had described my mother and her own mother's relationship. It was different though; my grandfather had been a prisoner in

Germany, and my mum did not meet her dad until she was five years old.

They were living in fear. I was probably not the mum my parents expected me to be. After these three months spent in France, I figured out my next move: Brisbane. I was scared of being judged in France or maybe I did not want to face myself. Whatever my choice, I knew that my family would always love and support me.

There are a few reasons why I chose Brisbane. Gary and Cyndi were incredibly supportive. I was still in love with Shane, and I did not want to see him everyday. I needed to move on. Secondly, with Shane's schedule, I wanted to avoid him popping up randomly to see Victoria. I wanted him to make her feel special when he was with her. He was always so busy. We did not do alternate weeks. I always said he could see Victoria anytime he wanted to. It was not about a week on or a week off, he was seeing her as much as he could and wanted to.

Victoria had a beautiful upbringing, alternating between the visits to her dad, her stepmother and siblings in Sydney, and then later in Melbourne. We made it work. Communication was always the key with Shane; we managed it well. His parents and sister were very patient; they still have an extraordinary place in my heart. I had my doubts as a mother. Should I let Victoria go live with her father? They were a family; we were not. Was I good enough? One heated conversation with Shane was regarding my private health insurance. He put Victoria on his card with his new spouse, and got me a single membership; the cost was significantly lower. I was so stubborn, yelling at him, and accusing him of taking everything away from me; my dreams, my life, and now my family. It was hard for me to see my private health insurance card with only one name written on

Motherhood

it. I know it was silly, but I was trying to rebuild a family, and I was angry and unreasonable. Once again, he was patient and compassionate, and waited for me to calm down.

Victoria travelled a lot with her dad; she went skiing on a regular basis. She went to Disneyland when we were living in South America. We flew with Victoria from Cayenne, in French Guiana to Miami. We had double nationality. Victoria had her Australian passport, and she was also on my French passport. I did not think that at the time, Australians would need a visa to enter America, compared to French Nationals who were not required to. We entered America on a French passport; and she would leave on an Australian one. I spent over two hours explaining the situation to the officer; in the end, they granted her a visa on her Australian passport. Oh, the joys and the beauty of travelling; this is how memories are created. Her dad also visited her in France, and she used to translate for him. On one occasion, they wanted a ham sandwich, and she could not remember the name for "ham," so she asked for a pig sandwich. I could write another book regarding our misuse of the English language throughout my life in Australia.

My second child was very different. I did plan to have her, as opposed to Victoria. I thought I was ready. Before giving birth to Jill, I miscarried on my way to Australia, on the plane. The agreement with Victoria's father was to come back to Australia; that was my promise to Shane. After two years spent in South America, it was time to go back. Jill was a beautiful, healthy baby. She was born in a sack, as my water never broke. I thought it was going to be a long birth like Victoria's, but no, my goodness! The first contraction started at 6 pm; I dropped Victoria off to my neighbour Judy. We arrived at the hospital by 7 pm; I asked Serge to park the car in the street, as the hospital car park closed at midnight. If that birth was going to be the same as Victoria's, we were in for a long night. But as usual, Jill was in a hurry; she bolted into this world. Within an hour and 15 minutes, she was born.

She was a red, healthy, beautiful baby. Victoria was excited to have a little sister. Serge also was excited. He has always been a good father

Birth of Jill.

Jill was easy going, happy and already independent. I was breastfeeding her and expressing a lot of milk. But she preferred the bottle and at 11 months, she was not interested in staying on my lap anymore. She was doing her own thing and had an adventurous nature. She loved Deedee. We had to put Deedee to sleep because she had a burst spleen, due to cancer. During Jill's early years, we were trying to open a new business, and I probably was not as relaxed and free to take care of her. But I did my best at the time. At the age of two, she was abducted by her dad. We got her back within three months, and I believed she suffered from this separation, which induced anxiety. I never wanted to talk about the issue of her abduction, as I did not want her to feel like a victim. I still remember everything as if it was yesterday; the way I felt when I learnt that she was gone, and the day I saw her again. Until now, I carried the guilt that I had somehow failed to protect her, on too many occasions. Does it create insecurity? She was the youngest out of the four girls, and her brother was born three months after her return from the abduction. She went from being the centre of attention, to the annoying little sister; the middle child syndrome.

I used to put her on the "thinking steps," and she would say: "Yes, no problem," and she would go pick up her toys. I had to tell her: "No, you can't move from your step, and you can't play. You're punished." She could stay for four hours sitting; she did not mind it at all. She has a strong character and she is always the winner, but at what cost? She can always get anything she sets her mind on. She is great.

My third child, David, is my favourite boy. He is the only one in the family who can carry the name. So much pressure on his shoulders!

While I was pregnant with David, Jill's abduction happened. It was a stressful time. The good thing was that I did not get morning sickness with David. He was a very tiny baby: 2.1 kilograms. It was a rapid birth, which only lasted a couple of hours. I did not have time to get changed, I just had time to take off my undies. The midwife broke my water, and here he was. I gave birth to him at 2 am, and was back home the next day for lunch. The kids came to visit me at the hospital before school. My second husband did the drop-off and came back home. The house was full of guests; my mother-in-law and one of my second husband's friends were there. I was back at home, cooking for eight people.

David was an extremely easy and beautiful baby. I breastfed him until he was 18 months. I stopped in February, as I wanted a rest for my breasts before having my next baby in June. He had the most prominent eyelashes, and the same blue eyes as his father. He looked like his cousin Gregoire, Eric's son. When he saw him for the first time, he was shocked.

David is the child who spent most of his time in hospital. He had cysts like his mother, accidentally sprayed bleach in his eye, scratched his cornea at the supermarket, and was diagnosed somewhere on the Autism Spectrum. Well, who isn't? We are all a bit autistic, aren't we? ADHD and various infections… You name it, he had it. He was the only boy amongst the girls. I understood his frustration. After 14 years of having girls, we could finally see blue belongings around the house, not just dolls and pink teddies but cars and balls. In my humble opinion and experience, it is remarkably interesting to witness the differences between raising girls and boys. His first word was "up." He had four sisters who could not wait to carry him. As a result, he did not walk until he was 15 months old. Still better than his grandfather, who walked at 18 months. He has never been interested in sports, but as a mother, you want all your children to find a hobby that they like. My first two girls looked like their respective fathers. I could not wait to have someone who took my side of the family. David looked like a Fortin.

Mia arrived after David. I wanted to have them close. She was born in June and was a very cute baby. I wanted to have a water birth, thinking we had to be quick to run the bath because the last two deliveries happened very quickly, in just under two hours. We went in the tub at the birth centre and after two hours, my second husband was getting very cold. The poor thing was melting in the bath! I wanted to stay in there, but Mia was not ready to come out. She was turning around a lot. We were wonderfully comfortable in the bath, going through the contractions. The nurse called the doctor; the birth was not progressing as planned. He broke my water, and Mia, like Victoria, was born with the umbilical cord wrapped around her neck. A couple of days before the birth, she was in breech position. My midwife gave me this curious advice: to put an ironing table between the floor and the sofa, and lay myself head down close to the floor, to try to turn the baby. The result of this potentially dangerous experiment: a baby still in breech position, and a broken ironing table.

When Mia was born, all the kids came to say hi to their sister. Everybody was excited. We were going home to a full house. We now had six kids at home. The following week, my second husband left for work on the Gold Coast. I had six kids, two on a part-time basis, and they attended four different schools. One was in high school, one in primary school, and the other one to another primary school. Plus two babies: David and Mia. And we all had our hobbies and duties: trampoline, music, drama, driving, feeding, and cleaning. People were always commenting on my organisation, but it did happen gradually though. The more kids you have, the more effortless it becomes. You get used to it. It is called planning.

> *"Failing to plan is planning to fail."*
> **Alan Lakein**

I had always wanted a mini-me, someone who looks and acts like me, and Mia does. We have the same eyes, the same temperament; we are people pleasers. Hopefully, I will be able to guide her through my mistakes. She was always more adventurous than her brother in sports, always very active and sporty. She learnt to swim early, and by the age of 18 months, she could cross the pool on her own. I felt very blessed.

I breastfed Mia until she was three years old. This was a very privileged time, a bonding moment between a mother and her daughter. I had to stop, as I was going to France for my parents' 50th wedding anniversary. In 2020, I missed their 60 years wedding anniversary, thanks to Covid-19. Each time she passed a milestone, like crawling or walking, I would get emotional and nostalgic, as it was my last baby. No more nappies, and I was looking forward to not doing them anymore.

And we did it; we did it very well. I was frustrated and tired sometimes, but it was good, and rewarding. There were a lot of arguments between the stepchildren and their step-mum. Ah, the love and hate feelings for the step-mum and the step-dad! But we all grew together as a family, and I did my best. The values I was brought up with pressured me to be the perfect mother and housewife; to cook healthy dinners, and make them clean their rooms. But I felt like a robot, mechanically doing what was expected of me.

Last but not least, is our Stormy. We already had six kids at the time. One member of my second husband's family was having issues with his child. Storm was placed in a beautiful foster family, in NSW. My second husband and I looked at each other; six or seven? What was the difference? We were both back at work full time. Mia was three years old, and we offered to be her guardians. We thought that our little Mia would be able to reassure her. We had never met her, and a week before she arrived, we had only seen one photograph of her. She had been in foster care since the age of 3 months, and Jane and her family had taken great care of her. She never crawled, but was always sitting and dragging herself forward with one leg first, then the other behind her.

I did not want to foster, as I knew I would struggle to give her back. Storm looked like a lost puppy. What she went through was sad; she was taken away from her mum and dad, and placed in a stranger's house. She was always pulling her hair; she had a bald patch on the back of her head. She was very shy and insecure. Out of my 7 children, she was the escape artist. It was quite interesting to see how we take for granted the love of our children. But when you foster, or when you adopt, you must earn their trust. Storm did not like to be touched, so I used to do baby massage to connect.

Motherhood

I learnt about baby massage when Victoria was born, while I was in Sydney with Debbie. Talking about this course, it was during this class that Debbie and I realised that our kids had started to get chicken pox.

Mia and Storm were jealous of each other; it was the only time she used to let me touch her.

Mia is a very affectionate child, and because she loved being touched and cuddled, Storm wanted the same thing. She could tolerate my touch; I believe the connections through the baby massage when she was little had helped her develop a sense of confidence.

It was funny, because she never moved away from me and was never more than a metre away for the first six months. We tried to build her trust; it is always fascinating when I was just assuming that she would be exploring, just like the other kids. I had tried to bring up seven children. You can have many guidelines to educate your children, but every one of them is different. As caregivers, we need to be flexible and resourceful.

Storm was an escape artist. She always loved animals. She did not want to spend much time with human beings. We always used to laugh; she loved talking to the ants in the backyard and observing the worms. Storm's favourite game, as a little girl, was hide and seek. Before leaving for school drop-off, I had to check all the seven bedrooms and try to guess which bed or quilt she was hiding under. It used to take me an extra 10 minutes. Sometimes, she would just disappear. She would open the side door and was taking the dog to the park, with just a singlet and a nappy. I was busy getting five or six kids ready for school; school uniform, lunch box, and breakfast. I'm sure some of

you can relate to how hard it is to make sure they all had their library books, their swimming and sports uniforms, and their music equipment; all this with your last child, a toddler, running around everywhere.

A couple of times, our neighbour brought her back, like a dog. On two different occasions, the police was called. One particular night, we had a roast dinner with Robin and Mick, Mia's godparents, and my girlfriend Nadia. They went home after dinner, and I sent the kids to bed. We spent some time with Nadia, cleaning up the kitchen. Storm was not tired as I had picked her up at 4.30 pm from kinder, and she was still asleep then. There was no chance I was going to put her back to bed at 7.30 pm. As usual, I let the dogs Oly and Jessie out, to the park. At some point, Storm told me that Jessie, our 15 years old dog, was back. There was no trace of Oly. I tried to reassure her, and said that Oly was younger, and that he would be back soon. But she still appeared very concerned. I finished the clean up, went to turn off all the lights, and check on the kids. I asked Victoria where was Storm. She replied: "I don't know. Isn't she with you?" I said: "Let me check again." I double-checked all the beds, and could not find any trace of Storm, and Oly. They were inseparable. Victoria was very distraught.

We went all over the place, and still couldn't find Oly. That's it, I thought Storm was gone again with Oly. I asked Victoria to look after the kids. I tried to listen to dogs barking in the street, like I usually did. No barks. Quiet. Still. My first reaction was to take the car, and within 30 seconds of doing so, I stopped, and decided to call the police. I explained the situation, and two police cars arrived with two or three officers in each vehicle. The first thing they did was to go inside and check every corner of the house, and when I say every corner, that included the freezer too. I tried to explain that I had already checked everywhere in the house, but they still had to follow the protocol, and the set rules for cases of missing children. This is the first thing they do: look inside your house. I remember saying: "She is not inside, can I please go look for her?" But I was not allowed to and had to stay with the police officer. Can one of them come with me to try to find her? I could not go anywhere. I was so frustrated, feeling useless to just be waiting there.

Victoria was in tears. I managed to keep it together for a while. They wanted to go public; missing children, Facebook, and AMBER alert. I kept telling them she was somewhere close with Oly, that she was not very far. I knew that she was with the dog. I told them over and over that: "If you find the dog, you'll find my daughter."

They started knocking on every door in my street. My beautiful next door neighbours were deaf. Police officers tried to knock on their door, but of course, no answer, as they were unable to hear. They were asleep. It was going to be a long night. I thought to myself: what a great start!! You must always try to see the funny side of everything.

It was now 10 pm, and still no Storm. 10.30 pm, and still no Storm. 11 pm, and still no Storm. At 11.10 pm, the phone rang. It was the police head quarters; they had received a call. A man had phoned, as he had been awakened by the barking of his dog. "I have a little dog in my front yard, with a little girl. She's young." It was only two blocks away; it was my Storm. The police went to pick her up, and she came back with Oly. She just told me: "Oly needed to see his friends, he was missing them." So, she took him to see another dog. And that's how she got lost. I had happy tears; a much needed tension release. It was, for

both the police and I, a Happy Ending story, featuring Stormy, my escape artist.

Another time, I was bringing the laundry upstairs and she put a stool against the front door to escape, again. We had a special code for when she was escaping. As soon as it was called out, it was the beginning of a search party. Everybody was on alert; Storm had escaped again. We all started running everywhere, dropping everything we were doing, and tried our best to find her. One lady stopped her car in the middle of the road, and we ran towards her. Before I could say anything, she started telling me how incompetent and irresponsible I was. How dare I leave my child by herself, with only a dog? She finally told me that Storm did cross the road just before, and someone else indicated that she went to an abandoned house. I kept calling her name, but only Oly turned up. I could not find Storm, but I knew she was somewhere in that backyard. I just knew it. I still could not find her, and after ten minutes, a guy said: "I saw her. She did not go out, she is still in there. I've been watching. She's here somewhere." I finally found her, hiding under the laundry tab, beneath the house. I opened the door, and peek-a-boo! No wonder I have so much grey hair and my ex-husband doesn't have any hair.

The third escape happened when I had to pick up David from Chess Club at 5 pm. Parents, I am sure you can relate to my experience. I had five kids at home, the oldest being 16 years old. Victoria was doing her own thing in high school, near the city. Jill, David and Mia were enrolled at Oakleigh, and Storm to "Mother Duck" in Alderley. The driving was hard work, especially with sports, trampoline, drama, chess and taekwondo. You just name it, they tried everything. One day, I had Jill, Mia and Storm at home, and I was emptying lunch boxes, and checking homework.

Motherhood

Storm needed to do her reading eggs on the Ipad, and she, for once, was very motivated. So, I asked Jill, who was 11 years old, to help her. Mia was watching TV. None of them showed any interest to come to the car when it was pick-up time for the other kids. I know it was not responsible to leave the kids by themselves, but my neighbour was aware that I would be gone for ten minutes maximum, and I called her as soon as I came back. Six minutes on the clock later, I was back and parked the car. David announced that he had forgotten his iPad on the bench, outside the school where he was waiting. U-turn and off we went to pick it up. Jill, hearing the car in the garage at home, went to her room. Mia was still watching TV. Storm was on her Ipad and accidentally landed on a different page. She was having trouble going back to her work page, and went outside looking for me. Within six minutes, I was back, except that, on my way home, I saw Oly at the park. I raced back inside and screamed: "Where is Storm?" She had gone down the road, trying to find me. So many things can happen in six minutes.

Jill and I started having an argument, during which I told her:

"I left you in charge."

She replied: "These are your kids, I'm not old enough to be responsible."

I answered that this was part of growing up; taking small responsibilities for six minutes at a time. But there was no time to argue. We needed to find Storm. "Search party, kids!"

Jill has always been very direct and brutally honest; she didn't sugarcoat anything, compared to her sisters. I found her a bit rude sometimes, but she was only saying the truth, and I didn't want to hear it. We looked around, and Storm was nowhere to be found. Some of our neighbours called the police to report that they had seen a child wandering by herself. Another mum recognised Storm, and was taking her back home in her car. The police had been called, and they came straight to my door. I explained everything, and justified myself again. Could I be neglecting my children? Oh my god! I was being questioned. I know I am not perfect, but being questioned by the law made me feel horrible. Out of my seven children, I never ever had a single one like her.

Social services also arrived. They asked me how they could help, and I said: "How about you give me an hour of babysitting during pickup time? It will just be fantastic!" "No, we can't do that," they replied. I then said: "Well, in this case, you can't help." My second husband was still away for work. We all have our struggles, but I always believed we were going to be fine, and I gave my best. As a mum, I am far from being perfect, but I know one thing for sure: I love my children to the moon and back.

I also was, and still am, a stepmother, and it was a different challenge altogether. I remember having a conversation with my older step-daughter after she left the house to live her own life. She apologised for being such a "b…" with me but it did not matter, as she was still a child. She had laid down the path for her siblings.

I feel privileged to have them all in my life. I believe children always choose you as a parent. I just want to say thank you to all of them, for choosing me. For being resilient enough to live with my craziness. Like one of my fellow authors said in her book "The Unexpected Journey:" "When you are expecting a child, you are told it is a trip to Italy, and sometimes you end up in Holland or Belgium, or somewhere in between. What is important is not the destination, but the journey.

Chapter 6

My Cancer

What is my relationship with cancer? It has always been around; my grandparents, my sister, my uncle, my friends, and my dog had all been affected by this pernicious disease. But it does not define us and we need to learn how to live with it. This chapter is dedicated to "Love your Sister," the amazing cancer foundation based in Australia. How uplifting to see Sam's hard work while I was going through my own cancer journey. Sam Johnson on his unicycle and Connie are still, to this day, an amazing source of inspiration. Thank you, from the bottom of my heart.

When I was a little girl, my grandma, dad's mum, had a mastectomy at a relatively young age. When we visited her after the surgery, she said something that stayed with me for a very long time. She told me that it was better to remove the whole breast, than have a lumpectomy, as the cancer would come back.

Virginie

After I saw her scar, I told her: "Don't' worry, it will grow back." She survived, until she turned 72.

Another significant encounter was with dad's colleague's daughter; she had broken her leg while playing soccer. While in hospital, she was diagnosed with bone cancer. Mum and dad invited their family over for afternoon tea. It was very awkward, as I had never met them before. Her mother asked her to show us her amputation from the hips; she was going through chemotherapy at the time. We were devastated when she died at the age of 10.

Françoise's dad was also sick, and he had pancreatic cancer. He eventually passed away, and when we went to his funeral, Eric's wife wished her wedding had been as joyful as Françoise's father's funeral; what a celebration of life! My friend was only 13 years old when she lost her dad. I can never imagine losing mine, even though I am now 51.

My Cancer

I lost all my three grandparents in less than twelve months. I was 17 years old when my grandpa Roger passed away from pancreatic cancer. My grandma from dad's side had breast cancer first, and then developed lung cancer, which deteriorated into terminal cancer. Her husband, my grandpa, succumbed from a heart attack; all of them within 12 months. I was very fortunate to have had enjoyed their company until the age of 17. Prior to each of their deaths, I always had a nightmare or a sign, letting me know the sad news before I even received the "phone call."

These intuitions and premonitory dreams have always been a part of me. It feels like I am constantly protected by angels. I imagine my parents or relatives thinking: "Which medication is she on? What is she smoking?" But I promise, I don't take anything. I have been incredibly lucky and privileged throughout my life.

My uncle, dad's older brother Pierre, also had cancer on his bottom cheek. At that time, there were only 100 known cases around the world. The surgeons cut a cyst and the end part of the little intestine, and he is still alive today. He is 87 years old.

My grandma France died of bone marrow cancer. She was still walking in July, and by August, for my wedding, she was in a wheelchair, and died two months later. She never had any chemotherapy. She was in her 87th year.

At 19 years old, I had a terrifying nightmare about my brother Emmanuel. He died of a rapid death on his 45th birthday, from an illness. In that nightmare, he told me he was there to warn me, to save me. It was horrible, and felt so real. I have always been close to Emmanuel because we shared the same passion for fencing. I am so proud of his achievements. I started checking on Emmanuel often, scanning his eyes, the colour of his skin, checking his lifelines on the palms of his hand. Bear in mind I did not know how to do palm reading, but I was still checking to see if he was healthy or not. After Emmanuel and Catherine's 45th birthday, I was reassured. Their birthday was on the 7th of June.

But at the end of June 2011, Catherine was diagnosed with cancer. She drove herself to the hospital, and they found a tumour on her kidney. She did not call mum or dad until she had the results and the diagnostic. I had it wrong the whole time. The dying person in my dream was not my brother, but my sister. She had kidney cancer, and the tumour on her kidney was 13 centimetres long. It is called the silent cancer because, when you realise you have it, it is already too late. She was 45 years old, and a mother of two beautiful children, Lucas and Quentin. After her diagnosis, she spent seven months with us. When my father told me the news, I was devastated. I remember falling to the floor. I called her and she was extraordinarily strong. I told her she could not go; with whom was I going to argue? We were so different; she was pretty and she had brains. I was sporty. We always had this sibling rivalry between us; we love each other dearly, and are still here for each other, but our relationship has always been conflictual. We were always team tagging; Emmanuel and I were the fencing team, Catherine and Eric were the readers, the intellectuals. Eric and I were the adventurous, the twins were the sedentary.

Although I was far away in Australia, I was still regularly talking to her over the phone. I remember telling her she had two kidneys and even if the surgeon removed one, she would still have the other, and she would be ok. But she was only given six months to live from the time she was diagnosed.

The doctors said she had metastasis in her lung and her bones, but I did not understand much about it.

She was in so much suffering. We encouraged her to go on holidays with Laurent, her partner at the time, and told her to be positive and live life, but it was too painful, and she had to come back. In August, she needed another surgery to consolidate three vertebrae, as she also had bone cancer. One night she got up, and this was the last time that she walked.

She asked my parents if they were able to look after her, as she was living in the country. They organised medical assistance at home;

there was an incessant venue of nurses and physiotherapists, and long hours of chemotherapy, as well as visits. Mum was exhausted. Dad was the master of organisation, and mum was the master of caring. I can understand why she wanted to be home; when you know the quality of mum's cooking, you don't want to go to the hospital.

I made two promises to my dad. When I asked him not long ago if he remembered anything about it, he said no. I did not want to promise anything, especially to dad, if I knew I could not follow through, but part of the process for me was to hear them before fulfilling them. On the 1st of July 2011, I promised I would quit smoking, and until today, I have never touched another cigarette again. The second promise was to write my book. Here you go Dad, this book is for you.

In 2011, I was working in the Human Resources department of a nickel mining company located in Brisbane and New Caledonia. That particular time was hectic; my second husband was working for the army, away in exercises in Shailer Bay. I was going back and forth to New Caledonia, and Storm, our 13 months baby girl, was due to arrive home to us on the 5th of August. We had a nanny, but life was still a bit chaotic. Work was quite intense too. I still managed to travel to France in November to spend ten days with my sister. We had an end of life celebration dinner during which I told my nephews: "Do you know I'm here to say goodbye to my sister? Next time I will be back, it will be for her funeral." They looked at me as if they did not believe me. I guess you only hear what you are ready to listen to, and they were far from being prepared. They must have been thinking: "Who does she think she is, to be talking like this?" I was known to be the silly auntie from Australia. And silly is precisely the word I would use at the time to describe myself.

My Cancer

It was such a sad few days. I remember going to the shops with her to buy some cigarettes. I had no choice but to give in to one of her last requests. She was on morphine. She tried to smile, but deep inside she knew. She was the exact opposite of me; when I wanted to fight and scream to cancer, (just like Sam Johnson would say: "F... cancer!), I would resolutely say: "You will not get me." But my sister chose to stay quiet. She chose to fight a silent battle. We went shopping; I realised how lucky we were in Australia, as the infrastructure was better suited for people with reduced mobility, as compared to Europe. She just wanted to be with mum and dad.

A couple of memories during these visits still resonate with me to this day. The first one was that my sister did not want to talk. She was always telling a joke, and she was exhausted. Even if she was sick, she put on makeup and perfume every day. Not that she needed any; she was so beautiful. To this day, mum and I still wear her perfume everyday. It is called "Jungle." One day, I bought it for a girlfriend, Tracy. She liked it so much that she wore it to bed. All her excitement vanished when her husband told her she smelled like me.

It was frustrating for Catherine to always ask for help for almost everything, including going to the toilet. She was frustrated with mum, and mum wanted to fix her, but she could not. She became paraplegic, and her self-esteem spiralled to a worrying low. We did not care; we still loved her. We always had a problem in our family regarding pride. Too proud to ask for help. With her challenging situation, certain questions needed to be answered. When my parents asked her how she wanted to be buried, she said she wanted a coffin standing up in the ground, which was impossible. Oh, I forgot that impossible was not a French word. It was a joke; everything was a joke. We always had a very dark sense of humour in our family.

Mum and dad were overwhelmed as they navigated the logistics of organising their own daughter's funeral.

At some stage, she needed radiation therapy because she had metastasis on the brain. She said: "Do you know what the worst thing is? You lose all your hair, your eyebrows, your eyelashes, but you still have your moustache." Until the end, she never lost her sense of humour. She was still entertaining, and I suppose it was a habit to take everything lightly in our family. Laughter is always an effective coping mechanism, even when situations are serious. My mum always used to say about dad: "Une merde dans le Sahara, et tu mets toujours le pied dedans," meaning: "Dad will always find a way to step on the only puddle of poo in a desert!" It is quite an embarrassing joke, but it was told with a lot of confidence. We love making jokes, we speak our mind, and sometimes we speak too fast.

While Catherine was asleep one day, I read her medical chart, which was about palliative care. I asked my parents: "Do you know she is in palliative care? That means she is going to die." My dad asked me if I was a doctor. I felt that he was angry with me. I was there only for ten days; it was easier for me to have a clearer head, as I did not live with them every day. I was not a permanent witness of my sister's suffering and the incessant roller coaster of results, doctor appointments, diagnostics, added to the cycles of not eating and hair loss. I had another perspective on the matter; I was living in Australia, unlike my two brothers who went on alternating weekends to help mum and dad, visit my sister and keep her entertained. As for my parents, like for any other parent, it is just horrible to see your children fade away at such a tender age. It goes against the logic of life to have to bury your own children.

My Cancer

Another memorable episode was when we used to go get lollies at the little supermarket next to the apartment. We wanted to watch a movie; we were taking our time at the shop. I was pushing her around on a wheelchair; we were making jokes, enjoying every moment together, knowing they were the last ones. There were four of us: my sister, one of my daughters, Victoria, mum and I. We were waiting at the disabled cashier, and it was 6.30 pm. It was the only wide space to push the chair through. People had just finished work, and it was peak hour; they had to pick kids up and head towards home after a long day at work.

As we started to queue, the cashier asked us to pass in front of everyone. We told them we had plenty of time and we could wait. We did not want privileges, but they insisted, and because Catherine was on a wheelchair, we had to go. The clients were furious and insulted us. I was in a state of shock; I was unable to speak. My sister turned around and looked at them, and shut everyone's mouth; she was not going to let them mistreat us. Cancer would not stop her. She still refused to let others walk over her feet. Well, technically, they could not because she was on a wheelchair. This distasteful joke is typical of the wicked sense of humour which ran in the family.

Back in Australia, I went back to work. Catherine's condition was deteriorating at a rapid pace. I was still travelling to and from New Caledonia. My mum and dad were supposed to visit us that Christmas 2011 but they cancelled the trip because they were looking after Catherine. In February 2012, after my regular monthly trip to New Caledonia, we were invited to the wedding of our beautiful friends, David and Anne, in New Zealand.

On Sunday night, I called my parents in France before going to work. Catherine was not doing great; she was going back to

Virginie

the hospital the next morning, on Monday. She was originally supposed to go back on Thursday, but had asked mum and dad if she could spend the weekend at home. I asked dad to let me know if there were any changes. Dad always wanted to protect us, and wanted to spare us the suffering. I was going to travel to New Caledonia for work from Sunday night, and I was due to fly at 6 pm. I arrived there at 1 am, and left at 5 am to catch the ferry, in order to be on-site by eight o'clock on Monday morning. Work until Thursday, catch a plane, arrive at 7 pm, and on a Friday morning, we had planned to fly to New Zealand for this beautiful wedding.

When I came back from New Caledonia, I called again to enquire about her; she was in hospital, in a coma, since Monday. I said: "I won't go to New Zealand and come straight home." My parents said: "No, please go to the wedding. We will let you know." So off we went to this beautiful wedding, and left the five kids with Dominique. New Zealand was lovely; we had such a lovely time at the wedding, which took place on an afternoon.

By the time we came back to the hotel, my then husband was watching TV, and I went on my iPad to check my Facebook. That is when I saw condolence messages regarding my sister. I knew then that she had passed away, but my parents did not call me, in an attempt to protect me. It is a big thing in our family, to protect each other. We try our best, but it is not necessarily the best thing to do. I was angry. I called them and they told me she had died. We flew the next morning and went back to Australia, with Emirates. I had a two-hour stopover, and I booked a flight and arrived in time for the funeral.

I arrived in Brisbane on Sunday night, changed my hand luggage from summer to winter clothes to suit the European climate.

My Cancer

And I was gone. I went to the funeral, arrived just in time to say goodbye, and to see her in the coffin. We said our goodbyes, and the funeral was beautiful. She was cremated. We took her back to my grandparents' tomb, with her kids and just close family members. My parents did not want flowers. They asked for donations for cancer. The next day, we went back with the urn to the hospital, and my dad had a very dark joke. Having carried her the day before, he said she was coming back to the hospital. It was not funny at all, but we all laughed. This is the sort of humour Catherine used to have. Mum was just upset with Dad, not amused at all. Anyway, they gave the donation money, hoping that would help alleviate someone else's suffering. She did suffer, and never complained. She died in February 2012.

While I was working in New Caledonia, one of our employees collapsed at work, due to a brain tumour. I had to organise his repatriation with his family, not long after he had passed away. Casimir and I went to the funeral in the Gold Coast; it was a beautiful ceremony. And yet another death from cancer!

In March 2012, I decided to participate in "Shave for a Cure," and donate my hair for a good cause. I raised over $10 000, and from this date, I have stopped colouring my hair. It was liberating. My whole journey had helped shaped my choices. I still had anger and resentment on the inside, but nonetheless, I kept growing.

Mum and dad visited us for Christmas 2012, and I miscarried in December 2012, which was interesting. Can you imagine us with eight kids? Anyway, we had a great Christmas, and I had received a reminder for a breast screening in 2012, but life was busy. Of course, I thought I was protected because I had breastfed my kids for over ten years; but that's just a myth. I was so positive that I would never have breast cancer.

Virginie

I did a mammogram when mum and dad were there in March 2013, and they left to go back to France on the 7th of March 2013, on Jules' birthday. He was one of my nephews. The breast clinic called back to have a follow-up mammogram. Nothing scary, as they had done the same thing two years ago. I had "a nice rack," as you would say in Australia. My breast tissues were dense. I was not worried; I could not find any lump. Nothing had changed in my breast, so I was confident. I took the day off on the 13th of March because it was Victoria's birthday, and I was supposed to bake a cake and have a small party at home. They kept me until noon for a biopsy; how inconvenient, because I had so many things planned. As mothers, we have our priorities, and I was never too busy to celebrate the kids' birthdays. At the end of the biopsy, they gave me an ice pack; a condom filled with water. That was quite funny, especially when I had to put it back in the freezer, and the little ones were asking all sorts of questions. The older girls had a giggle.

I went back on Friday the 15th for the results. I was riding my scooter. I worked in the city. I took the last appointment on Friday afternoon, and when I reached the lady doctor's office, she asked me if someone was accompanying me. I say: "Nah, I don't have cancer." Was I already in denial? Or was it positive thinking? She then took me to a room, where she explained that the results were abnormal. I said: "50/50 is not cancer." And she told me: "My husband is French." To which I replied: "Oh." Working at the French Consulate, I thought I knew everybody, but I did not. I met Jean-Michel eight years later with his wife. We had lunch with this lovely doctor and her family at a friend's place, Romain. What a small world!

"Abnormal," she said, and told me that I needed to book an appointment with an oncologist to have an open biopsy. Still in denial. A friend of ours, a nurse, told me to contact the first one on the list they handed me at the clinic, as they are usually the best in the eye of the referral doctor. I booked an appointment with the oncologist, Professor Ung, on Wednesday the 20th. I had to go in for a biopsy the following Wednesday the 27th. It was to be an open biopsy. It is similar to a breast lift; nine centimetres by four centimetres in width. Not an overly exciting procedure! The roller coaster of the cancer journey had started, and they warned me: "Virginie, you have to undergo quite a few medical examinations." I will not go into details about the costs involved when you have a private health insurance cover, and you think you are fully covered. This is another issue. Anyway, open biopsy, instant boob job, my left side was now facing north and the right side still south; apparently, it is called gravity.

My relationship with my then husband was not great at the time. We were planning to separate before my sister got diagnosed. Now, I did not want his pity because of my diagnosis. I was still planning to end the relationship. I was as proud and stubborn as ever.

But he was incredibly supportive. He accompanied me for my test, biopsy and mastectomy. We left at six o'clock in the morning and I returned the following week to get the results, and my husband was with me. But I got the days mixed up; I thought Wednesday was with the oncologist, and Thursday with the GP, but it was the opposite. The wait was the hardest; you must keep yourself busy. There was no point constantly worrying about it. Well, easier said than done. My husband was going to work; I went to see my GP for a medical certificate for work. And I asked her: "Is it cancer or not?" And she just said: "No, it's not cancer."

I can't recall who of my two brothers I called first. "Don't say anything to mum and dad until I've got the final results." I was getting confused; I was not sure if I had spoken to Emmanuel or Eric. Sometimes, your brain's performance tends to slow down. I did not want to hide anything from them, but wanted to protect mum and dad as much as possible. They had just lost Catherine a year ago. Did you notice this recurring family trend of always wanting to protect each other? Not necessarily a good habit, because if you start hiding the truth, it can ultimately backfire.

I remember having a conversation with my friend Bouchra: "I think I've got cancer." This was before my final results, and she warned me: "If you say you have it, it will manifest itself." I guess I underestimated the power of the mind. I told her about the premonitory dreams when I was a little girl. I always thought the dream was about my brother, but in fact, it was about my sister. Three weeks after her 45th birthday she was diagnosed with cancer and died. I think I knew I had cancer, and I also knew that I would be fine. But for me, my sister was there to protect me and tell me to look after myself. I feel so blessed to have my siblings who are always here for me; I am a little devil running around the world without much thinking.

Anyway, when my GP handed me the results, I used Doctor Google, because I could not understand half of the words of the report. I started opening multi-tabs on the computer, trying to dissect my report, which was full of complicated words such as Grade 4 and DCIS. It did not look too good. DCIS meant Duct In Situ Cancerous. My then husband asked me if I was a doctor. He said I was worried for nothing.

There was no reason to stress. I chose the denial approach, again. I called my parents to tell them what my GP had said: "No cancer," but I still needed to see the oncologist the next day. I tried to reassure them. I wished them a good night, and hoped the same for myself. My husband wanted to accompany me to the oncologist, as I had said I was not a doctor and my GP said it was not cancer. I told him I would go by myself.

So, on Thursday morning, I went to see my oncologist, thinking I did not have cancer. He asked me if I was by myself, and I said: " Yes, I do not have cancer." He then told me that the result of my biopsy was positive: I had cancer. "All your milk ducts have cancer cells. We need to book you in next week for a mastectomy." Even if I took it well, I was, to be honest, in a little bit of a shock. But maybe I knew already. Back to my dream when

Virginie

I was 18 regarding Emmanuel, I was prepared. We discussed a plan of attack, the first step of which was a mastectomy. Did I want a reconstruction at the same time ? No way! I remember what my grandma had said, years earlier. I asked if I would need chemotherapy, but he did not know yet. It would depend on whether the cancer had spread to the lymph nodes.

That particular phone call to my parents was the hardest thing to do. Usually, we spoke to dad to announce bad news, and he conveyed them to mum. We do not want her to get too emotional, but mum and I really are.

The first person I called was Rosa. I remember telling myself I should probably call my second husband to tell him. We were still fighting; I did not want his pity, I did not want him to feel obliged to love me with only one breast. From that point onwards, everything went terribly slow and exceptionally long, because between every appointment, was a whole and exceedingly long week. We tried to protect the kids as much as possible, because telling them the terrible news, knowing I had lost my sister a year ago, would be too much for them to bear. They asked me if I was going to die. I simply replied: "No, it is a different sort of cancer, and I had an early detection. I will be fine."

I had my mastectomy done, and it did not hurt too much. I had a visit from some fantastic friends, Cas and Anso. The entire list is way too long to cite here, but to sum it up, Rosa, Christine, Violaine, Lydie, Dominique, Bouchra and all my French family from Australia was here for me. The surgery was done on a Wednesday, and by Friday they wanted me to go home. I remember saying: "No, I've got one more episode of Star Wars to watch. I received the series as a Christmas present, three years ago and never found the time to watch it. Now was the right time. Could I leave on Saturday morning?" Bear in mind that we had six kids at home; I think I wanted some much-needed rest at the hospital.

I was waiting before calling mum and dad to let them know if I needed their help. I wanted to know if I had to go through chemotherapy or radiation first. I wanted them to be by my side if I was going through chemotherapy. They had only left one month ago, after having spent three months here, so I know it was a bit too much to ask for, financially but also emotionally. They took seven lymph nodes out of twelve, and they all came back negative. I was free of cancer.

On Sunday nights, we had a family dinner. I always made it a point to go downstairs, for us to eat as a family. Storm was three years old and still needed help to eat. We protected the kids so well that they did not help much. Did they even realise I had cancer? Nope, they were too young, too innocent, they must stay kids. My second husband was losing his temper; he was managing the house, working full time and looking after the kids at the same time. His frustration was building up.

"I did not want to hear any screaming and yelling." So, I went back upstairs. My second husband followed me, apologised and said: "I'm sorry, but they're not helping. I have to get it off my chest." I looked at him and said: "Actually, if someone's got something off their chest, it's me." And we just laughed. This wicked sense of humour! Maybe I should think a lot more before speaking... All my friends were so supportive. Every day, we had a homemade meal sent to us for eight people. I have been so fortunate throughout my life. Surround yourself with the right people; it will tell the story of who you are. Even if I did not need radiation or chemotherapy, I still asked my parents to come back. There is nothing better than to have your mum around, especially when you are unwell.

Three weeks after my mastectomy, I went back to work. In May 2012, I had Axillary Web Syndrome (Cording) and needed physiotherapy. I went back to work part-time. I was taking care of approximately 80 employees; some of them had had their contracts terminated. Work was hectic; it was the last year for most of my FIFO team from New Caledonia and the end of the contract. Exit interviews, repatriations, contract renewals for some: 26 pages in English, and 26 Pages in French. There was so much to do.

Finally, after three months, I was back to my old self, full of energy. Mum and dad's visa had expired. We went to New Caledonia; I was still on sick leave. I took some additional annual leave, and planned to take mum and dad for a week's holidays to New Caledonia. I had also decided to have another mastectomy, an elective one, for the right breast. My second husband was not happy, but it is my body after all, and I did not want any reconstructions. I was due to go back for surgery on the 10th of July; just an overnight stay and then back at home the next day. Mum and dad were always surprised at how quick we were leaving the hospital; I always felt I had experienced two extremes of the medical system. In France, they tend to over-medicalise patients, in my humble opinion. On the other hand, I love the Australian hospital stay. Especially considering I am not too fond of hospitals. As it was elective surgery, I thought I could do everything as my doctor had said, except I would still have the drain and I needed to rest. My body needed to heal. How silly I had been! I took my body for granted and put it through hell. I did not realise it at the time, but my body went through the same trauma, cancer or not cancer. It still suffered from the surgery, and I needed to take care of it, and nurture it. I went a bit silly with my dad, as I decided to change some of the wallpapers. I forgot to say that my second husband had surprised and renovated the upstairs bathroom while I was in New Caledonia with my parents. I remembered what one of my colleagues had once said to me: Two things in life can break your relationship: one is the SAP implementation, and the other one is renovating your house.

I came back from my sick leave, and the auditors from New Caledonia were waiting for me. All preparations for the audit were supposed to be organised by a support person, but nothing had been done. I was only meant to work part-time for a couple of weeks due to the mastectomy, and using the computer was not the best thing to be doing in my state. The first day, I did 9 hours of work, the second day lasted 11 hours. My second husband called me and reminded me that I needed to rest. I did not listen to him, nor to my body and by the end of the week, I had to go back in to see the surgeon. I had liquid buildup under the scar tissue. Every second day, the nurse had to extract about 200 millilitres. After a mastectomy, and before they can take the drain out, you need to have less than 30 millilitres of fluid per day, for two consecutive days, to allow for a successful healing process. My surgeon was not impressed, and I was back on the table. The drain was reinserted, and I was forced to rest for another two weeks.

After my second mastectomy, I still did not want the reconstructions. I chose to wear prostheses instead. As they needed to match my original breasts, they were massive!

Mum and dad went back to France in August 2013, after spending another five months helping us. They were exhausted,

Virginie

and I was in trouble with my brothers because mum was 74 and dad was 77. I think it was hard for mum and dad to take care of both the first and the second daughter. This had taken away two years of their life. At this age, it should have been the opposite. That was my very personal story with breast cancer. My cousin Jean-Yves also passed away from this disease.

I was following Sam Johnson on TV, and I saw the work he was doing with his beautiful sister. He was losing her to cancer and I had already lost mine. I was also battling my own cancer now. Sam, who I would go on to meet later on in 2019 when he came to Brisbane, did a fundraising road trip. I read his book and felt inspired. I felt he was angry like I was, and so passionate. I love the way he writes with Connie; I love Hilde, his sister; she also wrote a book. As Natasa put it: *"Sometimes, writing is more about healing than money-making."* I genuinely believe, from the bottom of my heart, that everybody should write a book. Even if it is just for your family or for yourself, please take the time to tell your story. I cannot wait to read it.

After my cancer, I was angry too; I wanted the world to know. I did some party planning with "Intimo," a lingerie boutique, to raise awareness on breast cancer. I wanted to prevent people from dying. I tried to save everyone: mums, sisters, and friends. October was breast cancer month.

With all my French family, also known as friends, we attended "The Weekend to end Women Cancer" in October 2014. Our team was called "O de Vie." Eau de Vie is quite funny because in French it refers to alcohol, but it also means *"water of life." We* walked 60 kilometres, and raised over $16,000. After the walk, our body never felt the same.

My Cancer

To my beautiful friends:

Lydie had a best friend who had breast cancer, and Christine had battled thyroid cancer. Blandine, Dominique, Karine, our speedy Gonzales, and Sylviane's sister in law were also diagnosed. Rosa was here because, after all, we are sisters at heart. Anne-Marie, Michel and Laurel have always been supportive of our actions. Carole, who had just arrived in Australia, had lost her best friend in France to cancer, and she was also a part of the team.

After 35 kilometres, we were still doing the French cancan in the middle of the night. The next day, we would keep walking.

Virginie

It was the most intense two days of my life. It was unique; it was beautiful. You have been there for nearly 30 years, you have always been supportive. Thank you for being a part of my life and for putting up with me. Our feet will never be the same again. One of my t-shirts had a photo of my sister. Rosa did it for me, and it was quite emotional.

A couple of years after giving birth to her daughter, Carole was also diagnosed with breast cancer. We loved chatting, and even though we never got to spend enough time together, we still enjoyed each other's company thoroughly. But we are forever bonded by this nasty disease. Cancer does not define us though, it just made us stronger. We are warriors, we are survivors.

I had been attending a support group at the Kim Walters Foundation at the Wesley, in Brisbane. For a long time, I thought I could go through this journey alone. But I was so wrong. You need the support of your sisterhood. I received a phone call from the foundation, asking me if I could help a French national who had just been diagnosed. She did not speak English fluently, and her husband was asked to stay in Australia for work. They had just changed their status from expatriate (where your health insurance was taken care of by your employer) to local employee, and they had two young boys. They had changed their insurance cover to the bare minimum. She was alone while her husband was working, and looking after the boys. Who was going to look after her? After my wonderful experience of enjoying my friends' support and them bringing food for the whole family, I felt compelled to help. A roster was organised to bring food over to her. It was funny to observe how I immediately tried to find a solution. My brain went on automatic mode straightaway: insurance, doctor appointments, hair shave, wigs, and the list goes on.... Sandrine went back to France, and her life changed for the better. We will forever be friends. She is inspiring, she is courageous, she is strong.

As I did not want a reconstruction, I opted for an external prosthesis. They feel soft to the touch and you can choose the size. I have never been shy, and I show them to whoever wants to see them. I have breastfed my kids for over ten years and I am quite sure I have uncovered myself in front of most of my friends. I loved breastfeeding and I felt comfortable doing it anywhere. Three years later, I decided to have a reconstruction. I was thinking of the practical side of things. You need to change prothesis if you want to go swimming. They also get quite hot in summer. I chose the breast silicone implant. I would have preferred the flap reconstruction but at the time, I did not have enough fat, and the recovery time was 18 months. I needed a quick process, as I still had to take care of the kids and work. The reconstruction is a personal journey, and surgeons, especially Susan, perform miracles, so to speak. I want to thank her and Chris for their support and beautiful care.

As my father said, I have never "mutilated" my body to fit into society; thanks to the values my parents raised me with, I did not even have my ears pierced. After three years, I needed to take the implants off, as they were feeling increasingly uncomfortable and I had developed scar tissue. Back to surgery again, and it was the best feeling ever; I was free, and could breathe properly again.

My journey with breast cancer is a very personal one. I love my body, even without breasts. It is quite liberating, actually. I am free. Free from the pressures of society, and the standards of beauty. My dad used to tell me that breasts were like hay for the donkeys. At my age, I do not want to waste my time with any donkeys anymore. My breast do not define me. I do not feel less of a woman without them. I feel full, I feel beautiful.

Virginie

My last words about cancer

Every morning, I tuned in to the radio, frequency 97.3 in Brisbane, and listened to Robin, Terry and Bob. On the 20th of March of this year, Robin was talking about her Sean, an inspiration, who had passed away. It brought back memories. These are some of Sean's words. One phrase stood out: "I am going to live with cancer, not die from it."

The second remarkable thing that he said was: "Imagine your life as a packet filled with a number of days. Each packet, in turn, is full of specific events: being born, getting married, and having babies, to name a few. The thing is, you can never know the exact number of packets you have in life. So choose to live the best packet of your life, everyday. Do not look for any extensions. Be happy, now." Thank you, Robin, for sharing this inspirational journey with us.

Chapter 7

My Journey, My Legacy

I am now 51 years old; my life, so far, has been a rollercoaster. I was constantly finding a million excuses to justify my way of life. I did feel guilt, but my unconscious justification was to live life as if every day was my last day. All my life, I have been pretending to be a good daughter, a good sister, a good friend. I was trying to fit into society. I was trying to follow the rules. I was pretending to be a good housewife, a good mum, a good cook. I was looking without seeing; I was listening without hearing. As Leonardo da Vinci said:

> *"An average human looks without seeing, listens without hearing, touches without feeling, eats without tasting, moves without physical awareness, inhales without awareness of odour or fragrance, and talks without thinking."*
>
> **— Leonardo da Vinci.**

Virginie

For my 50th birthday last year, I was considering different options on how to celebrate (one of them being hiking around the Mont Blanc with friends from Australia and Laure). Instead, I booked a two-day session at our local relaxation centre about non-violent communication. I still cannot believe I chose that over partying the whole weekend. But the thing is, I came to the realisation that I cannot communicate without getting frustrated and raising my voice. This session came as a revelation. I went on to complete a second course with Byron Katie, which was another enlightening moment. The third learning course was a week's transformation with Brendon Burchard. It was time for change to start happening.

I thought I was done and dusted with studying, but guess what? You should never stop learning. Everything and everyone around you is here to teach you something about yourself.

How many more failed relationships did I need?
How many more people did I need to hurt?
What was wrong with me?
Did I love myself?

I wanted to be happy, but how can you truly be happy if you are always pretending? For love to happen, you need to be true to yourself, you need to embrace your entire being, with your flaws and qualities. Can I love someone else when I do not even have self-love?

I must admit that, after writing my memoir, I finally realised that I did not love myself. I was constantly seeking external validation and trying to compensate for my own deficiencies and emotional needs through the love of others. Many times, I have fallen in love with souls who did not have love themselves.

I felt empowered to be a hero, their saviour, and I thought I could be the answer to their problems, and the light of their dark torments. I was focusing all my energy on listening, relentlessly working to make the other person happy. Yet what ended up happening was that I was mentally and physically exhausted. I had forgotten myself, I was a mere shadow of the person I used to be.

I have important things to voice out, especially for my children and their future life. What should they know about love?

A true love story does not hurt.

Love will only thrive daily when both partners become active and willing participants in their own lives, and when neither one of them seeks to only satisfy their own personal needs.

I realise that I have been wrong, all along. Well, better late than never!

My parents have been married for 60 years; they are my role models. Many times, I have wanted to copy them, but I did not witness how they had built their own story. All I knew was that they did not impersonate anyone else. Find yourself and believe in the universe; miracles do happen.

"I am an average human being, nothing wrong with that. I want to let my parents know; I am going to be okay. I am not scared to be alone anymore, and I love myself for the first time. I am not pretending anymore. I did what I did; I am who I am because I believe I needed to learn the experience. I am usually so black and white."

Virginie

To my children, this one is especially for you:
Remember that true love does not hurt. The bond between two people who decide to be together should be beautiful, comforting and wise.
The two statements "I love you" and "I love myself" should not contradict each other. Rather, they should always complement each other.
Remember to treat people the way you want to be treated.
Be kind to yourself and to others.
Know and love yourself.
Be true to yourself, and tell the truth because if you do not, then you will pay for it later, plus interest.
Thank you Helen for your guidance.
And last thing: live your life fully and keep an open mind.

In a mature relationship, I can affirm that: "I love myself" because I now understand that love and happiness will automatically happen when you feel whole, like a complete person who does not fear loneliness.

I cannot wait to live the rest of my life knowing, as Jean Gabin would say, that: "I know that I know nothing."

Finally, I will finish this book by citing a story that I love. Thanks to Casey, it sums up the new me.

Virginie

*My mum had a lot of problems. She did not sleep, and she felt exhausted. She was irritable, grumpy, and quite bitter. Her health was always so fragile until one day, where she completely changed, out of nowhere.
Our situation was the same, but she was different.*

One day, my dad said to her:

"*I have been looking for a job for three months, and I haven't found anything. I'm going out for a few beers with friends.*"
My mum replied:
"*It is okay.*"
My brother said to her:
"*Mum, I am doing poorly in all subjects at university …*"
My mum replied:
"*That's okay, you will get better, and if you do not, well, you repeat the semester, but you pay the tuition fees yourself.*"
My sister said to her:
"*Mum, I hit the car.*"
My mum replied:
"*Okay daughter, take it to the mechanic, find out how to pay for it and while they fix it, get around by bus or take the train.*"
Her mother-in-law said to her:
"*I am on my way to spend a few months with you.*"
My mum replied:
"*Okay, make yourself comfortable on the couch in the living room. The blankets are in the closet.*"

*All of us gathered at mum's house, worried to witness these unusual reactions. We suspected that she had been prescribed "I don't give a damn about 1000 milligrams" pills by the doctor.
Was she inadvertently ingesting an overdose?
We all agreed to do an "intervention" on my mother, in an attempt to remove any possible addiction she might have developed for some anti-tantrum medication.*

But to our surprise, when we all gathered around her, my mum quietly explained:

"It took me a long time to realise that every person is responsible for their own life. I discovered that my anger, my self-pity, my depression, my insomnia and my stress did not solve any problem. Instead, these feelings aggravated my condition.
I am not responsible for the actions of others. I am accountable for my own reactions.
Therefore, I have reached the conclusion that my duty to myself is to remain calm, and let everyone around me deal with their own demons.
I have taken courses in yoga, meditation, human development, mental hygiene and neurolinguistic programming, and in all of them, I found a common denominator: I can only effect change within myself. We have all been gifted with the necessary resources to navigate the intricacies of our own lives.
I can only give you my advice, if you ask me. Whether you want to follow it or not depends entirely on you.
So, from now on, I cease to be: the receptacle of your responsibilities, the sack of your guilt, the laundress of your remorse, the advocate of your faults, the wall of your lamentations, and the depositary of your duties. I refuse to keep solving your problems, or always being a spare tire to fulfil your responsibilities.

From now on, I declare you all independent and self-sufficient adults.

We were all left speechless.

From that day on, the family began to function better; everyone in the house was aware of their responsibilities, and we were all able to establish healthy boundaries.

Author:

A CONTENT WOMAN!

Virginie

About the Author

Virginie Fortin was born 51 years ago in France, in Châlons sur Marne. She is the daughter of Claude and Monique Fortin, the baby sister of Eric, Emmanuel and Catherine, and a proud mother to Victoria, Jill, David, Mia and Storm.

At the age of twenty years old, she migrated to Australia for her studies at the University of Technology in Sydney, which lasted nine months.

Always full of energy, she is a passionate and always follows her heart. At the age of 50, she realised that her train did not have the same stamina to keep running; she had run out of steam. She was mentally and physically exhausted. As the saying goes in France, she was burning the candle by both ends. It was time to pause. It was time to reflect. It was time to introspect.

You could not pin her anywhere; always running after new projects, and biting into life with a daring attitude. She is the explorer, the MacGyver of the family.

Virginie

Who will believe that she has written a book, her very own book? She never sits long enough to even read the newspaper!

She has made two promises to her dad. Back in 2011, she had promised to stop smoking and she has been true to her word. In 2019, she pledged that she would write a memoir. But how would she do it? Where would she start? She had never really enjoyed writing. Her family and friends have always been correcting her French or her English.

Words were not really her friends; she had always preferred numbers. Was she crazy? Or just very daring?

Be always careful with what you wish for. 2020 and COVID-19 proved to be the ideal moment for the gestation of her narrative. What a journey! She has stripped herself off, and uncovered intimate details of her precious life. She now understands the purpose of why her dad had encouraged her to write. What a liberating experience! Her dad is now eighty-four years old; good news that the book came to fruition. Life is so unpredictable.

48 hours of hard work which brought to life the start of a new beginning. This book is about her life. It reveals her dreams and depicts her colourful story.

References

Raising Children Australia. (2020). Retrieved from https://raisingchildren.net.au/pre-teens/development/understanding-your-pre-teen/brain-development-teens

Testimonials

My little sister Virginie should have been named "Sister Virginie," for she exemplifies love and kindness. She wears her heart on her sleeves, and is always ready to welcome everyone indiscriminately, even her worst enemy. She is bubbly and courageous, genuine and true to herself. She absolutely abhors any form of injustice, a trait shared by the whole Fortin family. Despite the trials and errors, she always finds the motivation to bounce back. She could have been in the humanitarian business rather than doing accounting; perhaps she would have flourished a lot more. But her life represents her choices, and when you are the mother of a tribe, it becomes important to refocus on the essentials.

Emmanuel Fortin

Virginie

I have been a friend and a spectator of your life for quite a few years now (25+?). There are a few adjectives that come to mind when thinking about you:

Loving, loving, loving; you are an incredibly loving person. You follow your heart and your instincts, for the best and for the worst. (Pour le meilleur et pour le pire).

Bold, brave and resilient.

An unwavering support to your family and friends.

Always ready for a good time with friends and a laugh.

Keep it that way. We love you as you are and whatever the lesson, we are willing to grow with you.

Bisous bisous.
Dominique Caron

It takes a lot of courage and tenacity to accomplish this project. A book, a real one!

Unlike in movies, life is not always a long, quiet river, but an adventure with counter-current ascents and detours. (Well, only for lives that have been lived to the teeth).

No doubt that the next adventure is already being written, literally or figuratively.
Rosa Dedaj

Testimonials

We met in 1998 during the famous Bastille Ball, sipping a panaché on the beach at Hervey Bay. You were a single mum then, and I lost sight of you for several years. When I found you again, thanks to Facebook, you went to French Guiana, and were married with seven kids. What an adventure!

I don't think you will ever stop surprising me!

Didier Beaudequin

Notes